A Club of One's Own
A Book Club Guide
for Starting and Leading Thriving Book Groups

Copyright © 2025 by BookBrowse

A Club of One's Own
A Book Club Guide for Starting and Leading Thriving Book Groups
Author and Publisher: BookBrowse
ISBN: 978-1-967264-03-2

All rights reserved. No part of this publication may be reproduced, stored in a retrieval system, or transmitted in any form or by any means—electronic, mechanical, photocopying, recording, or otherwise—without the prior written permission of the publisher, except in the case of brief quotations embodied in reviews, articles, or academic references.

This book is provided for informational purposes only. While every effort has been made to ensure the accuracy and usefulness of the content, it is provided "as is" with no guarantees of completeness, accuracy, or timeliness. The advice and strategies contained herein may not be suitable for every group or situation. The publisher and author disclaim any liability for outcomes resulting from the use or misuse of the material presented.

For information about bulk purchases, educational licensing, or special editions, please contact BookBrowse at:
www.bookbrowse.com

First Edition.

Table of Contents

Table of Contents... 2
Introduction... 6
   Why We're Writing This Book..6
   Why BookBrowse?...6
   How to Read this Book...7
   Why a Book Club?..7
   A Brief History of Book Clubs..9
Chapter 1: Starting or Joining a Book Club... **12**
   What Does Your Ideal Book Club Look Like?... 12
   Public vs. Private Book Clubs... 13
   Questions to Answer When Starting a Book Club...15
      1. When will you meet and for how long?.. 15
      2. Who do you want in the group?.. 16
      3. How many people?... 17
      4. How important is book discussion to your group?....................................19
      5. What do you want to read and how will you choose books?....................20
      6. Do you want someone to lead the discussion?... 21
      7. How many books do you want to read and how often do you want to meet?... 22
      8. Where will you meet?.. 23
      9. Does your group want to wait to read in paperback/cheaper ebook format, or even audiobook format?.. 24
      10. Will there be food at your meetings?..25
      11. How will you contact members?... 26
      Summary: What to consider when starting a book club..............................26
      What if you're leading an existing book club that hasn't aligned on all of these questions?...27
   Recruiting Members for Your Book Club...27
   What to Consider When Joining an Existing Book Club...................................29
   Common Concerns When Starting a Book Club..29
   Qualities of a Good Book Club Leader or Participant..31
Chapter 2: How to Run a Book Club Smoothly... **33**
   Set Clear Expectations...33
   Prioritize Direct Communication...34
   The Book Club Health Check..35
      What's the first word you would use to describe your group?.....................35
      Are the meeting frequency, time, and location(s) working well for everyone?..... 35
      Are there any issues to discuss relating to attendance and reading the book?..... 35

- Is everyone happy about the types of books being discussed and the process for selecting them?...36
- Is the size of the group working well?...36
- Is there a good balance between discussion time and social aspects?.................36
- What about the discussions themselves?..37
- Is the group's overall organization and communication working well?...............37
- Is there anything not already covered that members of the group would like to start or stop doing?...38
- Next steps..38

Chapter 3: Choosing and Sourcing Books..39
- How to Choose Books..39
- Buying or Borrowing — and Alternatives!..43

Chapter 4: Preparing for and Having Successful Discussions...................45
- Creating and Sourcing Book Club Questions..45
  - Writing Discussion Questions Yourself..45
    - Using Generative AI to Create Discussion Questions.............................47
  - Book Club Discussion Questions for Any Book!..48
    - General Book Club Questions..48
    - Book Club Questions About the Author or Their Writing.......................48
    - Book Club Questions Focused on the Book's Story.................................49
    - Book Club Questions About the Book's Characters.................................49
    - Book Club Questions for the Book's Setting..49
    - Genre-Specific Book Club Questions..49
    - General Book Club Topics Relating to the Book......................................50
- Preparing for Sensitive and Respectful Discussions..50
  - Resources...52
- Why Appoint a Facilitator or Moderator?..53
- Facilitating a Discussion..54
- Warming Up to Discussion: Icebreakers...57
  - Pass the Hat...57
    - Example Questions:..57
  - Pair Share..58
  - Wordplay...58
  - Quiz...58
    - Example Quiz..59

Chapter 5: Addressing Issues and Making Improvements.......................60
- Keeping Discussions Focused..60
- Dealing with Overly Dominant Personalities (ODPs)...60
  - Set time limits or take turns...61

    Communicate the problem to the group..61
    Give the ODP a job to keep them focused...62
    Communicate the problem to the ODP..62
    Discussions Straying Off-Topic..62
  Regularizing Attendance...63
  When People Don't Read the Books..64
  Improving Book Selection...65
    Take Turns...65
    Put It to a Vote or Discussion...65
    Organize a Schedule for Picking Books...66
    Screen Selections...66
    Expand Your Horizons..66
  Adjusting Group Size...67
    Group Too Small..67
    Expanding your numbers...67
        Expanding for diversity...68
        Integrating new members...68
    Group Too Big..69
  Cooling Down Competitive Hosting..70
  Confronting Problematic Members Sensitively and Asking Members to Leave.........71
  Why People Leave Book Clubs...72

Chapter 6: Virtual Book Clubs..75
  Why Go Virtual with Your Book Club?...75
  Tools for Online Book Clubs..75
    Private Groups for Posting and Commenting..75
    Group Text Chats..76
    Video and Audio Calls..76
    Suggestions for Hybrid Discussion...77
  Public Virtual Book Clubs..77
  Bonus Option: Postal Book Clubs..78

Chapter 7: Extra, Extra! Ideas to Enhance Your Book Club......................80
  Book Club Food Ideas...80
    Make Something Easy and Shareable..80
    Create Meals or Snacks (or Drinks) Based on the Book..81
    Support Your Local Restaurants...81
  Inviting Authors to Your Book Club...81
  Mixing Things Up: Add-Ons and Alternatives for Book Club Meetings....................83
    Attend a Virtual Author Reading..83
    Pick a Topic or Genre..84

    Share What You're Reading Now..84
    All the World's a Stage...84
    Take Inspiration From the Literary Salons of Old....................................85
  Even More "Extra": Fun Things to Do with Your Book Club.......................85
    Getting Out and Going Places...85
    Celebrating...85
    Volunteer and Community Work...86
    Enjoying Time Together in Other Ways...86

Turning the Page: The Possibilities of Book Clubs..................................87
  Book Clubs on the Rise...87
  Final Thoughts..88

Book Club Resources...90
  Accessing Support Group & Book Club Resources Electronically................90
  The Key Questions to Answer When Starting a Book Club...........................91
  The Book Club Health Check Template...94
  Book Club Discussion Prep Worksheet..97
  Book Club Facilitator Worksheet...100
  Example Exit Survey Email..107

Acknowledgements..108

Notes..109

Introduction

Why We're Writing This Book

Starting a book club, like any new venture, comes with the potential for both rewards and challenges. But unlike with many groups and activities, there seems to be relatively little detailed advice out there regarding the logistics of putting together, leading, and participating in book clubs. We hope to fill that knowledge gap by providing concrete ideas, solutions to problems, checklists, resources, and relevant perspectives to anyone thinking about starting or joining a book club, as well as anyone who could use help maintaining or getting more out of their current book group.

We also want to encourage and offer support to those going the book club route who need guidance and a confidence boost, as we know it can be an intimidating process. Whether you're feeling anxious about getting your club off the ground, experiencing problems with your current club, or just wondering if you can create a book group to suit your unique needs and preferences, we're here to help! But, you may be wondering, what qualifies us to give advice on book clubs in the first place?

Why BookBrowse?

While we don't claim to be the ultimate authority on the subject, BookBrowse has been active in researching book clubs for over two decades. During this time, we've collected and compiled data through surveys of tens of thousands of book group members and the general public. We've also conducted interviews with group leaders and participants for more than fifteen years, and gotten to meet a lot of wonderful people in the process. Plus, we host our own book club discussions online and regularly offer book club advice through resources available on our website and in our free newsletters. Through this book, we hope to continue our outreach in an engaging and substantial way.

We won't just give you dry, obvious pointers, but clear, proven approaches and personal anecdotes from real book club members to keep things fun and relatable. At the same time, our extensive experience with book clubs has made it clear that there's no one-size-fits-all formula for a club, and no limits to what a book group can or should look like. Any advice that we give in this book is intended to be flexible and customizable, and we intend to appeal to a wide audience with diverse and thoughtful examples that reflect how much we value the vast possibilities of what a book club can be and achieve.

How to Read this Book

We encourage you to read all seven chapters of *A Club of One's Own* beginning to end, but as we know book clubbers are often busy people, the table of contents preceding this introduction is broken out into detailed subsections to enable you to jump to whichever part of the book may be most useful to you depending on your circumstances. Leaders of existing clubs may be tempted to skip Chapter 1 (Starting or Joining a Book Club), however you may find the questions useful for increasing alignment and reducing friction in your existing groups.

Throughout the book we've included charts and tables to provide additional insights into our surveyed book clubs, and at the end of the book we've included templates for different book club resources, as well as instructions for how to access digital copies of these resources.

After you've read this book for the first time, we hope you'll return to it often as a trusted reference—whether you're troubleshooting an issue, planning a new initiative, or simply looking for fresh inspiration for your club.

Why a Book Club?

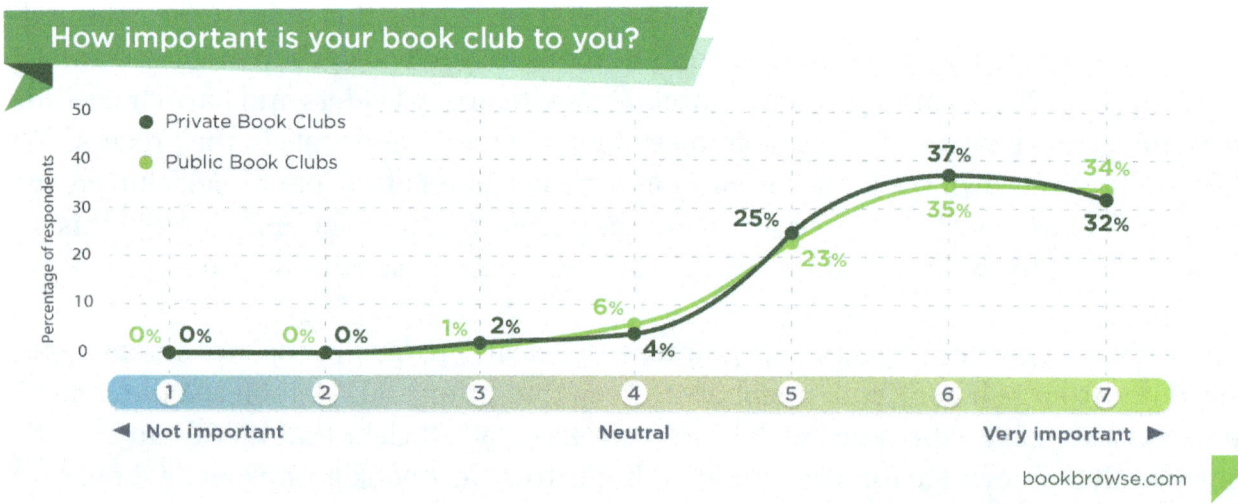

A book club fulfills a certain combination of social, emotional, and intellectual human needs, and can set the stage for immensely satisfying experiences. Reading is generally thought of as a private and solitary activity, but bringing it into an arena that involves other people creates an opportunity for internal reflection to become external. Book discussions give us a way to absorb stories while also sharing our personal stories with each other. They also allow us to introduce "deep" or significant topics in conversation that we might struggle to bring up in everyday social situations where small talk seems like the safe and expected route. At their best, book clubs create a comfortable environment for individually and collectively exploring ideas, feelings, values, events, and experiences that are important to us. And, of course, for broadening our reading knowledge and discovering new books and authors together.

In our work with book clubs, we've found that groups can have many other benefits, too. **Some clubs provide unique support for people with shared experiences and goals.** At Harrison Public Library in New York, Giovanna Fiorino-Iannace created an ESL Book Club[1] for participants who want to improve their English reading skills. Adrienna Turner started the C Facility Book Club[2] at Sacramento State Prison to help members strengthen their communication and public speaking and have the opportunity to develop critical and analytical abilities while in prison. Writers As Readers[3] of Rockford, Illinois convened to discuss books they felt would help them improve their craft. According to founder Vicki Moore, the self-explanatory Zoom Black Girls' Book Club[4] began in part as "a response to the many challenges the coronavirus pandemic has brought to the African American community."

Book groups can also create an opportunity for members to indulge in a particular focus or interest. In the Books for Cooks[5] cookbook club, affiliated with Martha Washington Library in Alexandria, Virginia, members came together to share their love of cooking, recipes, and food culture. Some clubs use shared interests to foster connections and form gatherings that might not otherwise exist. The Cross/Over Book Club[6] of Wichita, Kansas, for example, focuses on YA books and is open to both older and younger members.

Regardless of the reason behind a club, **members sometimes find their book group to be a strong source of community that lasts years and even decades**, and many clubs use their power as a group to support causes they care about, making a genuine impact on the world around them. New Jersey-based club Sistas Are Reading[7] has participated in and organized multiple fundraising events, and has arranged scholarships for young women. The Bibliophiles[8], also in New Jersey, has banded together to take political action and raised money for the United Negro College Fund.

How long have you been in your book club?

Age	2 years or less	3-4 years	5-7 years	8-10 years	11-14 years	15+ years
35-44	31%	24%	21%	14%	5%	5%
45-54	27%	17%	18%	16%	12%	11%
55-64	21%	17%	18%	13%	14%	17%
65-74	11%	11%	24%	16%	12%	27%
75+	11%	11%	24%	16%	12%	27%

The sample size below 35 years of age is insufficiently robust to break out by age.

bookbrowse.com

Due to their intimate nature, book clubs can lead to lifelong connections and friendships. Amy Piper of the DC group Girls' Night In Book Club[9] told us, "You learn a lot about each other while discussing books. There are lots of friendships that have been made in our book club that are active outside of meetings...Most of us met each other via the book club and have become very good friends over the years."

In short, there are many great reasons to start a book club, and your club may turn out to offer further unforeseen benefits. Book clubs are a meaningful way to build connections with people you might not otherwise know, and can also be a vehicle for becoming immersed in the world around you in ways that you might otherwise not have imagined possible. No matter what your reasons or goals in putting together your own club, we want to support you!

A Brief History of Book Clubs

Since ancient times, people have gathered in various settings worldwide to share and discuss stories and exchange ideas. The book club as we know it today, which has developed alongside modern publishing and the availability of mass-printed literature, has in many cases addressed a lack of accessibility to education and community, and evolved in step with political movements and needs.

American sources often name the first book club founder as Anne Hutchinson, who began a group for women to discuss weekly sermons on a ship bound for the Massachusetts Bay Colony in the 17th century. This claim seems somewhat arbitrary — surely this wasn't the first time a group of people gathered regularly to discuss texts of some kind — but its place as an accepted historical first shows how we define book clubs in retrospect and how we still value them: often as a necessary resource for women, and frequently as a way of filling an intellectual, social, or educational gap. Hutchinson, a critic of Puritanism who was willing to challenge male religious authority, made an intellectual space for women in an atmosphere where they were not expected to take part in serious discourse (the group was condemned by others on the ship, and Hutchinson was later excommunicated from the colony for holding and teaching non-Puritan views).

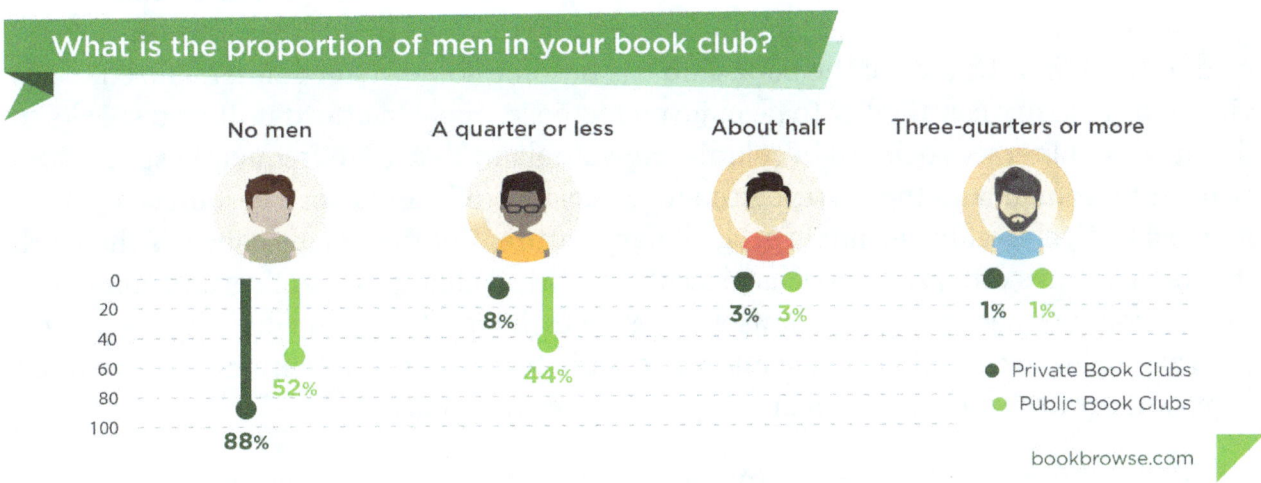

Throughout the 18th century and into the early 19th century, reading groups and organizations for women sprang up around New England. These clubs were predominantly made up of wealthy white women, but as early as the 1820s, free Black people in the United States were forming their own literary societies, including the Coloured Reading Society (in Philadelphia, for men) and the Society of Young Ladies (in Lynn, Massachusetts, for women). Groups like this, which fostered education, social support, and cultural life, were often active in the antislavery movement. With abolition came the expansion of Black reading circles, which helped cultivate an audience for Black authors and publications, and eventually contributed momentum to the civil rights movement.

In the 1920s, mail-order book clubs took off. At the time, books weren't as widely accessible to the average reader, so subscription clubs with a book-of-the-month arrangement were a useful resource. In the 1950s, as the availability of cheap paperbacks increased, a mailing list called the Cory Book Service provided people with a discreet way to receive queer literature, and created a community that paved the way for future LGBTQ+ book groups and the gay rights movement. The need for mail-order clubs decreased with the advent of chain bookstores in the 1980s, but they can be viewed as a precursor to today's large-scale book clubs connecting hundreds or thousands of readers that are often run by celebrities, influencers, or organizations. Oprah's televised book club, started in 1996, is responsible for popularizing this format and book clubs in general. In the meantime, private book clubs have continued to serve as places for building community, and as hubs of discussion and even political action.

Today, book groups are often portrayed cynically in popular culture as the domain of well-off housewives in suburban neighborhoods who use book discussion as an excuse to drink wine, gossip, and talk about their lives. This image makes practical sense considering that book clubs remain most accessible to those with disposable time and income, and that the idea of the book club has become somewhat commercialized, viewed as a luxury commodity to be enjoyed by those who can afford it. It also speaks to the history of literary societies in colonial New England that were frequently spaces for rich white women, and there are legitimate criticisms to be made of a certain type of modern book club culture and its exclusionary nature. But this image conceals the truth that book groups often still serve as places for political change, and in certain contexts the stereotype smacks of general misogyny, suggesting that women who get together to read and drink are frivolous and couldn't possibly be talking about anything deep, or are vapid simply for wanting to socialize freely in their own spaces.

What is certain is that book clubs still serve many needs, and probably even more than they used to. Based on publicly available data and BookBrowse's own research, we estimate that just in the US, over 13 million adults[10] participate in book groups. Today's book groups can be a place to discuss books, find community, make friends, learn about the world, organize for political change, indulge in gossip, and much more. Read on as we provide resources and advice for starting and running a successful book club.

Chapter 1: Starting or Joining a Book Club

What Does Your Ideal Book Club Look Like?

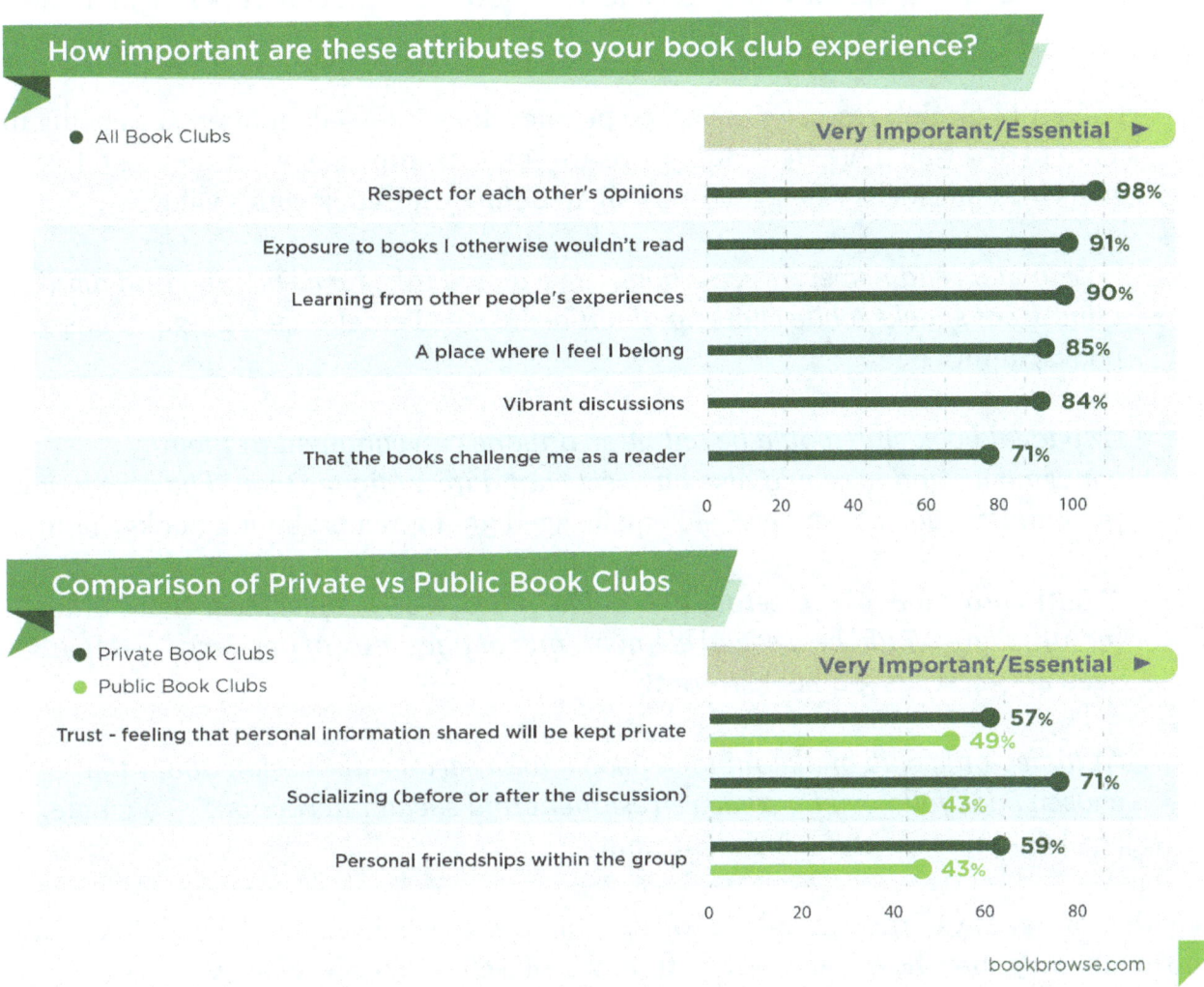

Many book clubs start when a few friends get together and decide they'd like to meet to discuss books. Beginning a club with your friends can be great, but keep in mind that they may not share your feelings about what books to read or how the club will run. Some clubs stay very focused on book discussion, others may touch on the book before moving on to general chat; some expect members to prioritize the book club, others are happy for people to drop in when convenient; some insist the book has to be read before attending the meeting, others don't mind either way. There's no right way for a book club to run, but what's critical for the happiness of the group is that members agree on some of the basics.

Many book clubs are made up of people of similar ages and stages in life, but it's interesting to note that groups that have a range of ages and/or a mix of genders often say how much they value the different perspectives. Before forming your own club, consider visiting other groups to pinpoint what's important to you. Many libraries and bookstores run book clubs, which are almost always open to the public and welcome drop-ins. These can be a great way to get a feel for how different clubs operate and how you'd like yours to be.

As part of our book club research, we asked people who expressed an interest in being in a book club to describe their ideal club. Here are some examples of what they said that might give you some ideas when you're trying to define your book club's values:

> *"We would read newer, diverse books. We would take turns hosting and drink wine & eat snacks while chatting about books!"* — Female, aged 25-34, reads 3-4 books/month

> *"My ideal book club would be online so anyone can comment at their convenience and we could also have set chat dates. Anyone would be able to join in no matter age or gender."* — Female, aged 35-44, reads about 2 books/month

> *"Multi-cultural books, meeting in a public place, 8-15 people, meet every other month, there would be a social element, mix of ages, mix of genders."* — Male, aged 45-54, reads 3-4 books/month

> *"A ladies-only club of like-minded people with serious discussion about the chosen book followed by some refreshment and social interaction."* — Female, aged 65-74, reads about 2 books/month

Whether or not any of the examples above resonate with what you think you'd like in a book club, they show how you can start thinking of a club in terms of size, demographics, meeting locations, and reading selections. In the next section, we'll explore some questions that can help you determine more specific preferences.

Public vs. Private Book Clubs

Many book clubs are private, involving gatherings of a select group of people. If you want your club to be invitation-only or to have close control over who attends, a private group is probably best for you. But if you don't mind new members showing up, or if you think of a book club as an interesting way to meet people, you could consider advertising publicly so that anyone — assuming they meet or adhere to any requirements set out — can join in discussions or other events.

You may already be considering a public club if you want the group to be attached to an organization, business, or public resource. Maybe you're a librarian looking to start a book club at your library, or a bookstore owner wondering if a discussion group could help connect your shop to the local community. Depending on how you want to arrange your public group, it may look different from a typical book club. For example, if you've gained a following through a podcast where you interview authors, an associated book club could be as simple as prompting your audience to read a certain book ahead of listening to a talk with the author. On the other hand, some public book clubs only fundamentally differ from your usual private club in how membership is handled. Like private discussion groups, public clubs can serve as a source of social support and a fulfilling way to build relationships with others.

If the decision of whether your club should be public or private isn't already determined by your circumstances, you'll want to consider how each option will shape the group. Those considering starting a public club may benefit from thinking about the following factors ahead of time:

- **Accounting for size.** Consider requiring people to reserve spots for a meeting or event beforehand. Even if you don't want to limit the number of people who show up, this will help you know how many attendees will be there and plan accordingly.

- **Rules and requirements.** Just because a club is public doesn't mean it necessarily has to be open to everyone, and rules can be even more important in a less structured environment. In a public club, it's crucial to consider what people need to know when attending a meeting as well as who the club is for, and to specify this on any public announcements. For example, is the club only for library members, women, students, etc.? Does everyone attending need to have read the book? Is there help available for obtaining a copy of the book, or do attendees need to obtain a book in a particular way (purchasing one from your bookstore, for instance)? Will there be any associated fees?

- **Leadership.** While public groups don't necessarily have to be run by only one person, close-knit private groups can provide an opportunity to share leadership duties (like facilitating discussions) between members, and to adjust expectations based on what members decide together. In public clubs, where membership and attendance might be more fluid, groups may benefit from a set format and leader so that attendees have dependable guidance and the club maintains a consistent atmosphere regardless of its makeup.

Questions to Answer When Starting a Book Club

Here are some questions to consider in the beginning stages of forming your club. They can be questions for you to think about individually before you start reaching out to others, but should also be useful for discussing between members as you figure out what sort of group is right for all of you. Your answers to these questions might change as things progress, but thinking about them early on will help you understand your priorities and nail down a plan for moving forward.

It's tempting to think that logistical issues can be worked out along the way, and to a certain extent, they can be. But being clear on at least some of the basics (like attendance, discussion time, and how meetings will progress) will help you start your club more efficiently and make the process more enjoyable.

1. When will you meet and for how long?

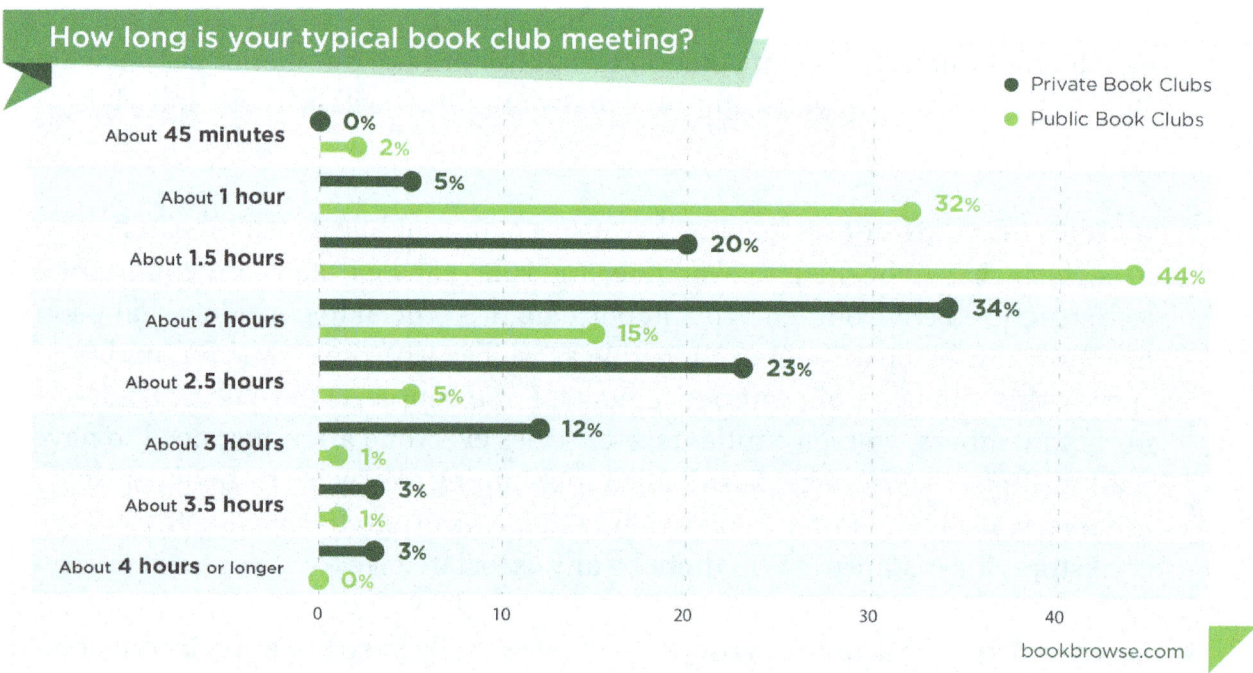

Most groups meet for an hour or two. Some meet during the day, over the weekend, or for breakfast. Workplace book clubs often meet at lunchtime.

Suggestion: Select a time that fits best with the schedules of most people in the group — and stick with this once chosen (e.g., first Tuesday of each month, 7 pm). That way, everyone knows this is book club time and can plan their lives around it, and you don't have to coordinate calendars every month. For a relatively relaxed meeting, aim for about 2 hours. For example:

- 7 pm: Arrive (meet, chat, eat — if food is on offer — and discuss any book club issues like what to read next).

- 7:45 pm: Open the book discussion.

- 8:30 pm: Close "formal" discussion, allowing plenty of time for discussion/chat outside of official book club talk before the meeting ends at 9 pm.

2. Who do you want in the group?

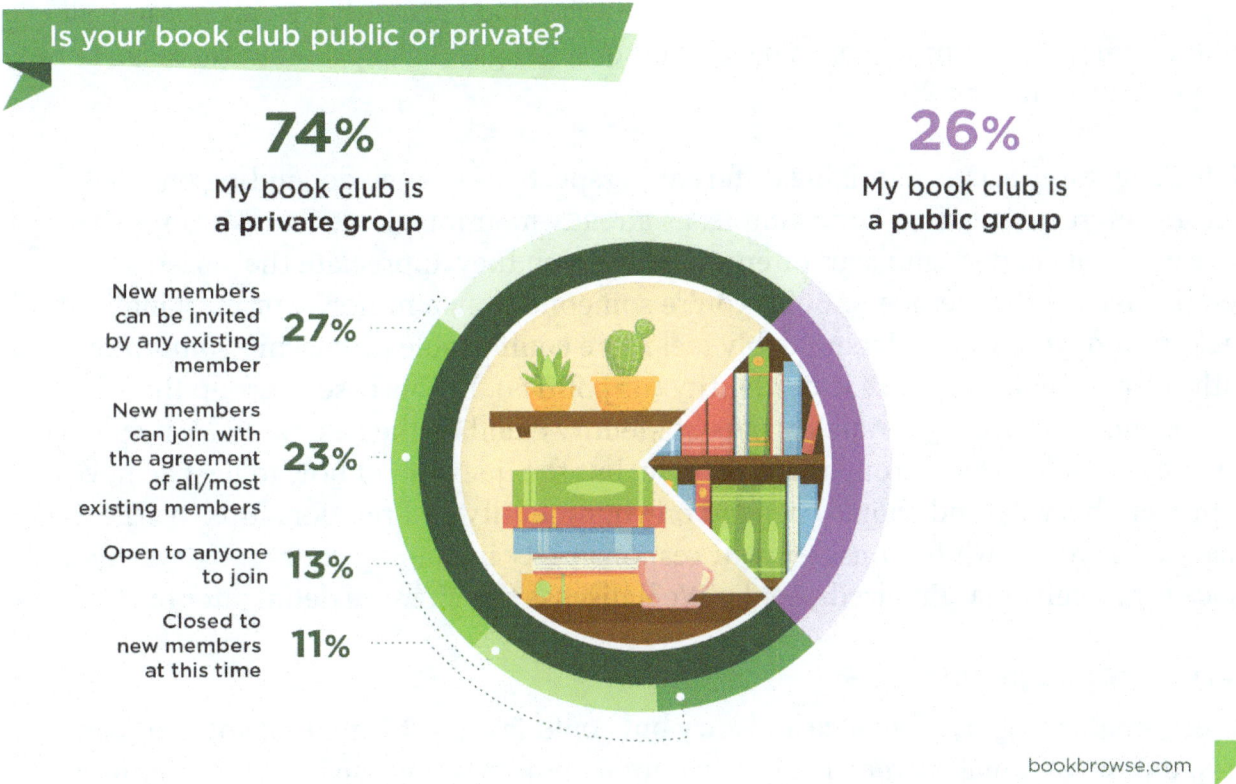

Do you envision your book club being limited in terms of gender, or mixed? Do you picture being surrounded by other people you can relate to and share experiences with? Or do you want to meet people who aren't necessarily in the same place in life, or who have had different experiences? Do you want people to be about the same age — or how about mixing different generations (like with a mothers and daughters book club)?

Many groups share common ground of some kind or other — for example, having met through their children's school — but there may be significant variations among them.

What is the approximate difference in age between your oldest and youngest member?

	5 years or less	About 6-10 years	About 11-15 years	About 16-20 years	About 21-25 years	26 years or more
Private Book Clubs	19%	31%	17%	15%	6%	11%
Public Book Clubs	8%	18%	18%	17%	14%	25%

bookbrowse.com

Suggestion: Either look for people with some common ground (e.g., all women, all couples, all 30-somethings) *or* make a point of mixing things up so that there isn't one person who stands out.

Note: The implications of mixing different perspectives change depending on what factors you're addressing. For example, as already mentioned, we found groups that have a mix of genders and ages often say how much they appreciate the varied perspectives of the members. But if you're someone from a minority or marginalized background, you may understandably feel more comfortable discussing your opinions with people you know share your identity (or politics). In this case, a group that's homogenous regarding certain aspects of identity could be the best plan. Many people say they would prefer a group that's diverse, but the question of how to best achieve or approach this will (and should) depend on your identity and relationships to others. For instance, if you're white, consider your responsibility in making your club a welcoming place for racially marginalized people. We'll discuss this in more detail later on.

3. How many people?

A very small group can feel nice and cozy but could fall apart if a couple of members drop out or can't make a meeting (or turn up without reading the book). A very large group *can* work but needs to be run on a more "formal" basis to ensure the conversation stays on track and everybody gets a chance to contribute.

Suggestion: About eight people is a good size to aim for. It's a small enough number to fit inside most homes or around a table in a cafe, and gives everybody a chance to voice their opinions. And if one or two members can't make it to a meeting, or drop out altogether, there are still enough people left to form a good discussion.

Remember, just as important as the number of people in the club is the number who actually attend the meetings. Most book clubs expect members to prioritize meetings. A big source of angst in many clubs is when regular attendees get frustrated because others rarely show up. One reason for the stress is that the no-shows are blocking the opportunity for others to join, and their absence means there are too few people to form a good discussion. Also, the group dynamics often change when the no-shows do turn up because they haven't invested the time in the group that the regular members have, and so the regular members don't feel comfortable talking openly.

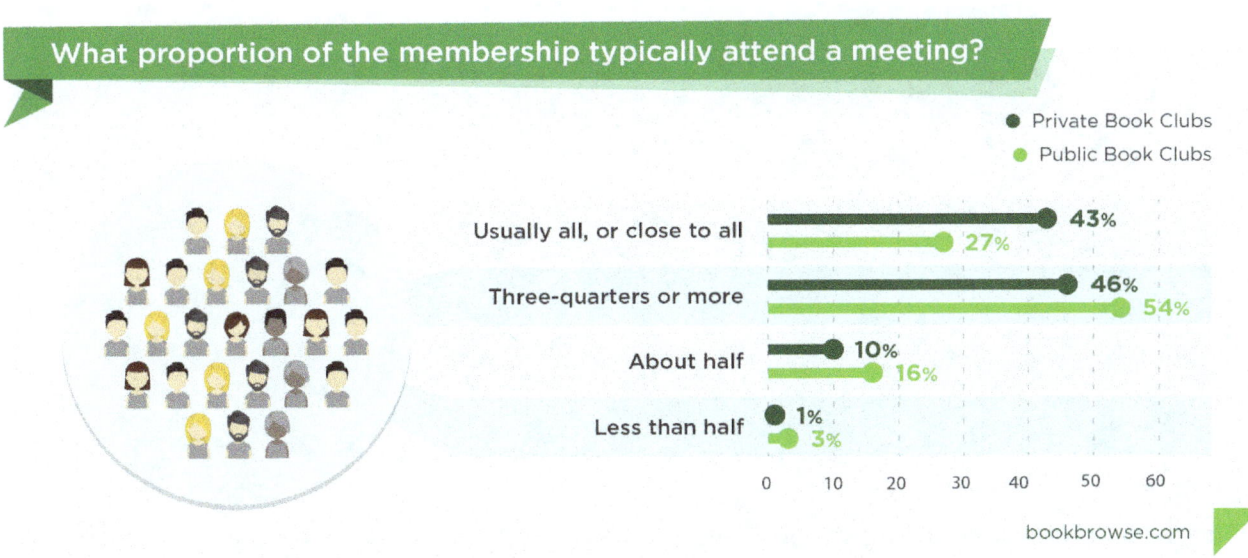

When starting out, if there's just a handful of you, it may seem silly to worry about your group's size. But what if each of you invites a friend, and then they invite friends? Before you know it, the group could be too big to be manageable. So take a few moments up front to agree what the optimal size for your group is and how new people can join (e.g., can somebody just bring a friend along, or do they have to consult the group first?).

4. How important is book discussion to your group?

On the face of it this question might seem odd. After all, you're getting together to discuss books, right? But differing expectations in this area is probably the leading cause of book club strife. If one person is expecting to spend the entire time in deep discussion, while another signed up thinking there would be token book discussion plus lots of chat, somebody's going to be disappointed. Another area of disagreement comes from members having different opinions on whether it's okay to come to a meeting without having read the book.

Suggestion: Find a happy medium. For your club to work, members need to make reading the books and attending the meetings a relatively high priority — but if somebody can't attend from time to time or doesn't always get a chance to finish the book, it isn't the end of the world.

Typical time spent on book discussion by length of meeting

Approximate Time Discussing → Length of Meeting ↓	30 minutes or less	40 minutes	50-60 minutes	75-90 minutes	2 hours or longer
1 hour	15%	23%	62%	-	-
1.5 hours	13%	17%	46%	24%	-
2 hours	14%	13%	34%	35%	4%
2.5 hours	18%	14%	29%	28%	11%
3+ hours	12%	13%	26%	35%	14%

bookbrowse.com

Most book clubs socialize first and then get down to discussion. Decide what will be best for your group and try it for three to four months, and if it doesn't work, try something different. Aim to discuss the book for about half an hour to start and see how it goes. Keep an eye on "off topic" conversations but don't be rigid — many of the best books allow us to reflect on aspects of our own lives and these reflections can lead to really interesting discussions.

Generally speaking, we've found in our research that people enjoy groups that make substantial time for discussing books. Among groups that spend 75 minutes or more on discussion time, 81% of participants described themselves as "very happy" with their book clubs, while in groups that give 20 minutes or less to book discussion, only 55% say the same.

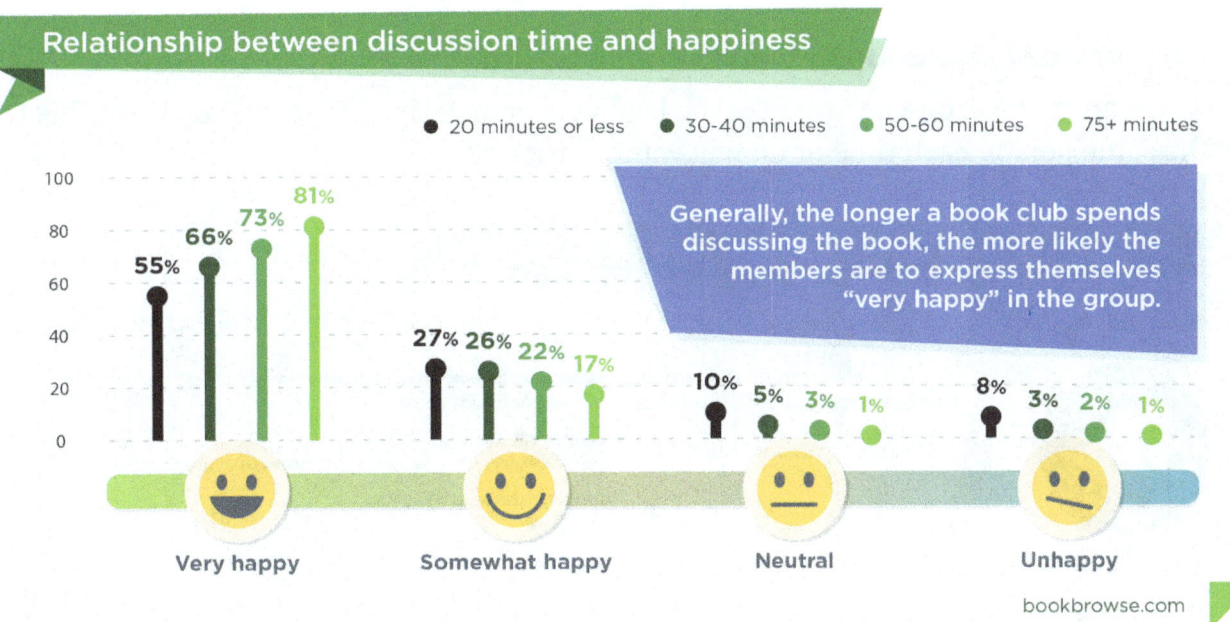

Whether the group is large or small, encourage all book club members to read the book and attend the meetings regularly. This is particularly important with small groups as it's discouraging when barely enough people turn up to form a conversation, or too many haven't read the book, making it difficult for the few who have to discuss it. If you find members are regularly not reading the books, then maybe the book club isn't for them or your group needs to reconsider the types of books you're reading.

5. What do you want to read and how will you choose books?

Some groups only read a particular type of book, but most groups read a wide variety of genres.

Suggestion: For the first couple of books, if your book club isn't already based around a specific focus, try established book club favorites (in the realm of popular literary or historical fiction, for example — and these can cover quite a lot of ground). Of course, these aren't for everyone, so make adjustments as you see fit, and remain open to possible changes depending on how things go.

Most book clubs read fiction the majority of the time, with novels that explore contemporary issues and historical fiction being favorites, but the vast majority of clubs read across a variety of genres at least occasionally — from nonfiction to poetry, fantasy, and mystery. If you want to set a theme, try it for a maximum of two or three books and review how it's going after that. The range of possible themes is endless — books in the news, award winners, South American authors, books about travel, graphic novels, etc. — and may be very personal to a club and its members. Many book clubs require the person recommending a book to have already read it — which is a great rule!

6. Do you want someone to lead the discussion?

Do you want to have one person take the lead at each meeting? If so, do you want this to be the same person each time or do you want to rotate?

Suggestion: Even if your members are used to being part of group discussions and are good at listening to each other, it can still be helpful to have a nominal "leader." For many groups, this role falls to the person who recommended the book being discussed. The role of the leader is, in part, to make sure that everyone's voice is heard — e.g., to gently redirect the conversation if it goes too far off-topic. The best way to do this is to have new topics ready to suggest, which brings us on to another important job of the leader — to come to the meeting with some thoughts on what topics would be good to discuss, so if the conversation starts to run dry in one area, they can redirect to more fertile areas.

As already mentioned, book groups that devote more discussion time to a book tend to have a higher percentage of members who are happy with the club. Our research also shows that having a facilitator tends to correlate with longer discussion times.

Because all but 8% of public book clubs surveyed have a facilitator, the chart above shows private book clubs only.

bookbrowse.com

7. How many books do you want to read and how often do you want to meet?

Do you want to meet every week, once a month, every quarter? Do you want to discuss more than one book at a meeting?

Suggestion: Most book clubs meet once a month for most months of the year (maybe taking a month off in the summer and doing something different in December like a book exchange or get-together with significant others). And most book clubs discuss one book at a time. Your group needs to decide what's best for you, but it's wise not to get too ambitious. A good rule of thumb is to start with once a month and one book at a time, and keep the early books to around 300 pages or less. If you do want to discuss more than one book at a time later on, a
good way to do this can be to read on a particular topic — for example, everyone reads about a certain historical figure, but half of you read a biography and the others a novel, and then you can compare the two approaches as part of your discussion.

8. Where will you meet?

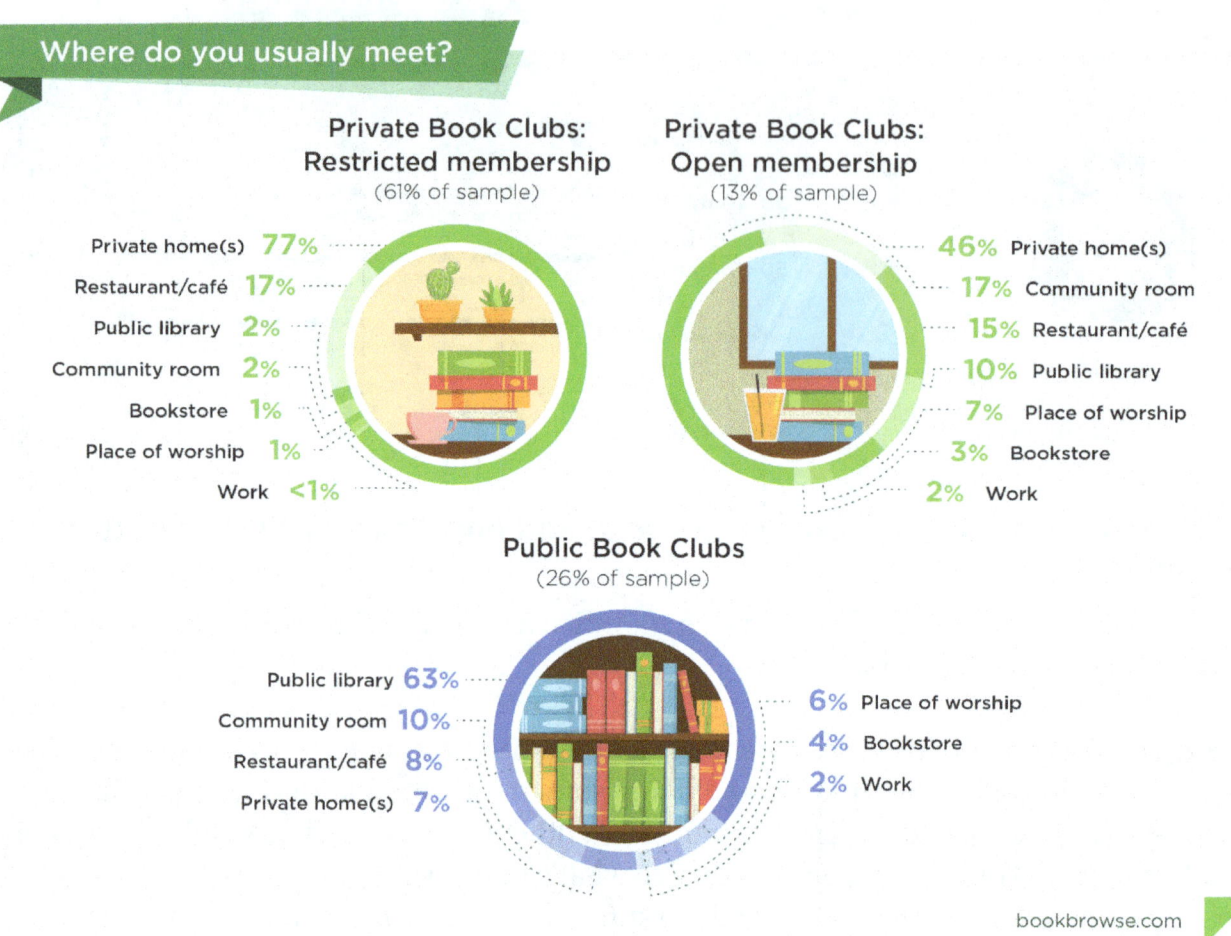

Do you want to always meet in the same place, whether somebody's home or a public space like a room at the library or a coffee shop? Or do you want to rotate around each other's homes, or meet in the same home?

Suggestion: If the people in your group already know each other, then meeting in someone's home may be the easiest option, but keep in mind that some people may not want, or be able to host a meeting at their own home — e.g., those with roommates or who live with family; whereas for other members — e.g., those with small children and no babysitter, it might be the only way they can attend. Be sensitive and flexible to each other's needs, and if you have an in-person club, consider making it more accessible by allowing members to attend virtually if they wish.

If you're starting a new group and some or all of you don't know each other, you may want to meet in a public place until the group is well-established. There are two reasons for this. The first is that this allows your group to get to know each other without being weighed down by the added pressure that could come from visiting one another's homes. The other is simply a matter of basic safety — you probably wouldn't invite a blind date to pick you up from your house, so don't invite a group of strangers into your home until you know them well enough to be sure you can trust them.

Meeting in a public place also comes with the advantage that nobody has to clean the house or prepare food — which can keep things simpler. What you choose very much depends on what works for your group. But if you're looking to grow your book club, your best bet may be meeting in a public space like a coffee shop, as this tends to be less intimidating for a new member than knocking on somebody's front door. If you want your group to be a mix of genders, and/or to include men, then you might also want to consider a public place: not only may this make everyone feel safer, but half of the men we surveyed who are interested in being in a book club (but are not currently in one) say they would prefer to meet in a public place — only 15% preferred to meet in a home.

One important consideration when meeting in a public place is seating. Generally book clubs meet in a circle or around a large table, but at a restaurant or coffee shop, you may not be able to seat a larger group at one table, or it may be difficult for one end of the table to hear the other. If you do decide to meet at a coffee shop or other public space, see if it's possible to reserve a meeting room or larger table in advance so that your seating does not negatively impact your conversation.

9. Does your group want to wait to read in paperback/cheaper ebook format, or even audiobook format?

Historically most book clubs would wait for the paperback to publish, but now with the rise of the popularity of ebooks and audiobooks many clubs will read books within a year of the original publication date. For example in 2024, two of the most popular books discussed that year[11] were published in 2024, with another published in December 2023. Even before ebooks were widely read, most would make an exception and read in hardcover occasionally.

Suggestion: Whatever format you decide to read, it's best to plan your schedule at least a couple of months ahead so members aren't scrambling to find and read books on short notice (40% of book clubs plan at least four months ahead). With a few months' notice and access to a reasonably sized library, it's possible most members could get their hands on a hardcover copy at no or relatively low cost — by borrowing from the library, buying books secondhand, or buying one copy and sharing it. And, of course, many book club members read ebooks or listen to audiobooks, which opens up other possibilities (audiobooks in particular can lead to their own discussion questions related to the narration as well). Having said that, waiting until the paperback is available (which also tends to coincide with a cheaper ebook version) tends to take the pressure off. There will likely be less demand for copies in the library and those who buy will be paying less. So we recommend planning ahead by at least two to three months and generally waiting until the paperback is available.

10. Will there be food at your meetings?

Do you want food to be an integral part of your meetings? Maybe you'd rather make it a low-key or even nonexistent element. In some groups that meet in homes, everyone brings a dish. Others have one person provide the food, and another brings the drinks. Some have the host provide a simple snack for the group. Some enjoy themed food — e.g., if discussing a book set in Italy, bring Italian foods. Some people like to meet in a restaurant — if you go this route, make sure you book a table in a quiet corner, and that the restaurant doesn't mind you chatting after the meal has finished!

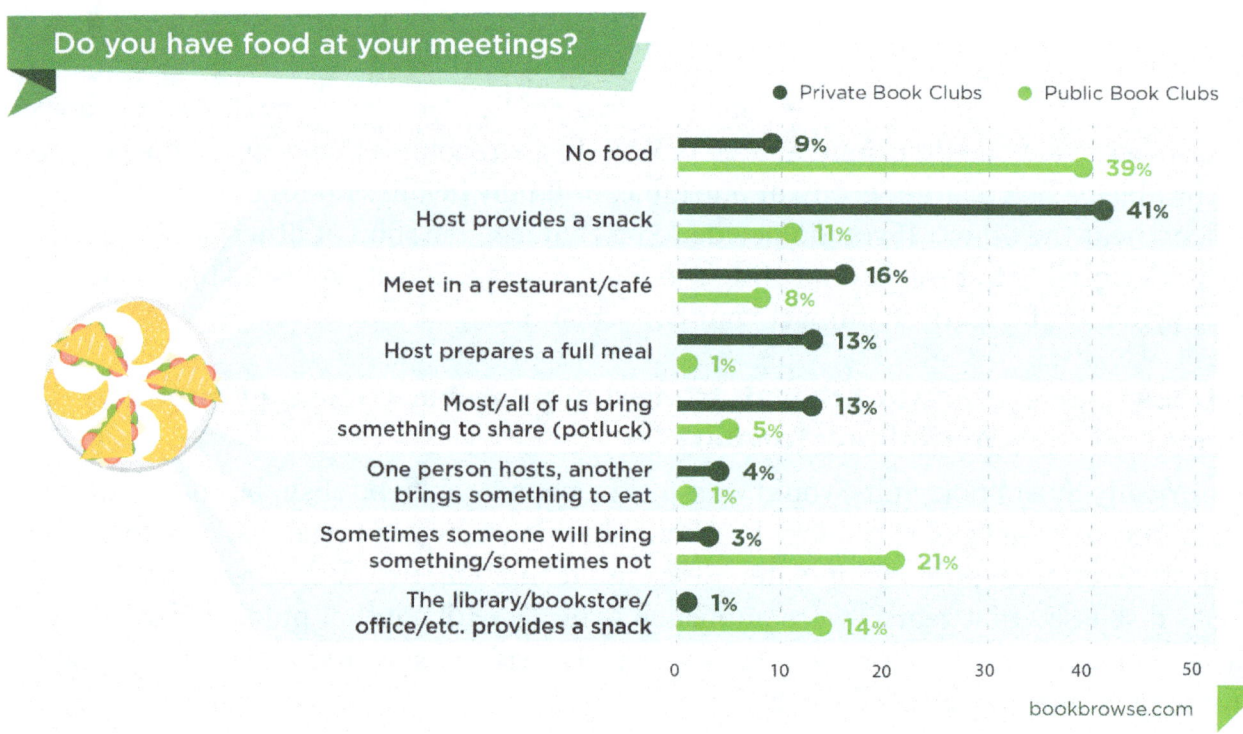

Suggestion: In general, keep the food simple and serve it at the beginning of the meeting so people can do their socializing first.

Along with food comes the question of beverages, of course, and alcohol can be a sticky subject for book groups and gatherings in general. Serving alcohol may alleviate discomfort for some but create discomfort for others. Make sure your group is on the same page about whether or not there will be alcoholic drinks at meetings, and that no one feels pressured to partake. Always including non-alcoholic options can help accommodate anyone who doesn't want to, or can't drink.

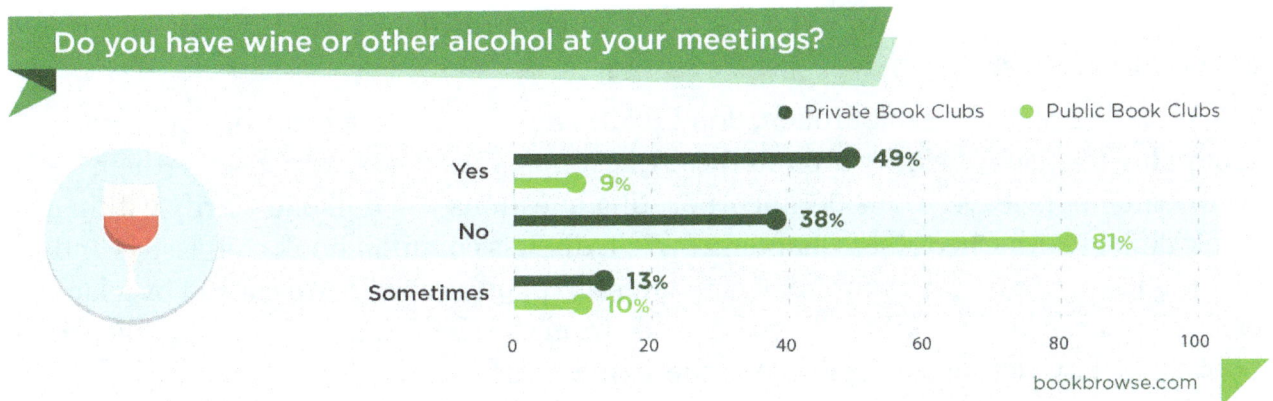

11. How will you contact members?

These days, most groups run on email, and this is a good way to reach people whether your club meets online or in person.

Suggestion: At the first meeting, if the event is in person, pass around a piece of paper and have people write down their contact information clearly — then type it up and email a copy to each member after the meeting. There are also online resources that help book clubs coordinate information and share book ideas (for example, Bookmovement.com[12] and Bookclubs.com[13]).

On Bookclubs.com you can create a club and invite members to join through email or text message before, during, or after your first meeting. You can post meetings and book polls and message members through the platform. When you do, all members will receive email and/or text notifications.

Summary: What to consider when starting a book club

Overall, aim to have a structure your book club agrees on, but allow for flexibility. What works for others may not work for your group. Stay focused on making the club a fun, comfortable, and interesting place to be, and whatever form it takes, it's sure to be a success.

That's a lot of things to be thinking about, but here's just one more! Unless you already know each other very well, before you even start discussing how your group will run, spend a little time getting to know each other. One way is to simply go around the group saying who you are, why you want to be part of a book club, and what expectations you have for the club. If this feels a little intimidating, try one of our Games to Break the Ice below.

What if you're leading an existing book club that hasn't aligned on all of these questions?

As the saying goes, if it isn't broken, don't fix it. However if there is tension in your group due to a lack of clarity around these questions, then it's best to discuss them before members leave. Consider incorporating questions you'd like to clarify within a Book Club Health Check (see Chapter 2). We'll discuss common book club issues and making improvements to your book club later on, many of which are caused by a lack of clarity on these key questions. As you can see from the chart below, many established book clubs have left one or multiple of these questions unanswered:

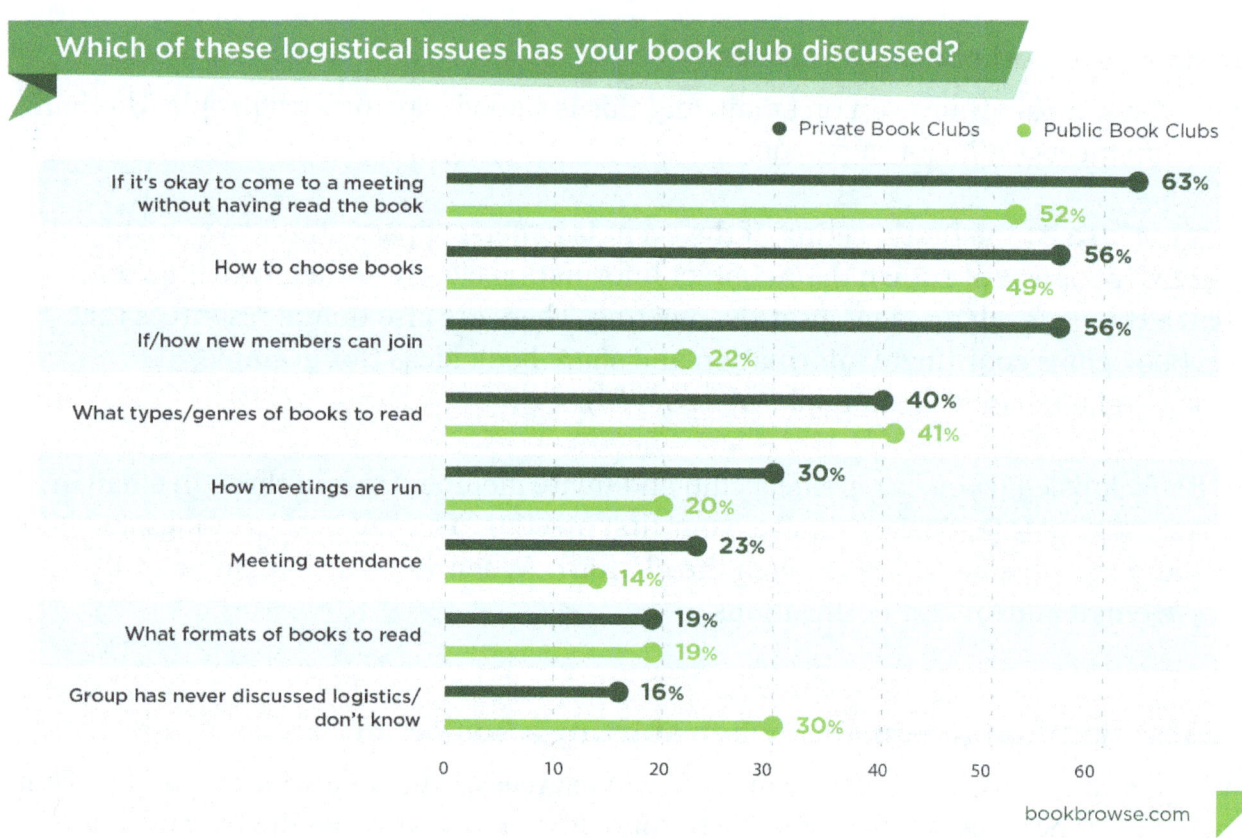

Recruiting Members for Your Book Club

You may already have people you can ask to join your book club in mind, whether specific friends and acquaintances or a general pool of potential members, like co-workers or neighbors. In the case of the latter, you can get the word out about your club by placing an announcement or sign-up sheet in a common area, or just asking around. But what if you don't already have a particular community or group in mind? Or what if you want to find people with similar interests related to books and discussion, but don't know where to look? Here are a few directions you might take:

- **Goodreads** is a popular resource for finding and connecting with other readers, and also offers its own platform[14] for organizing clubs (see more in Virtual Book Clubs later in this book).

- If you're already active on **social media platforms like Facebook, Instagram, Twitter/X, or Bluesky**, consider seeking out others in your area (or anywhere, if you're planning on a virtual club) to connect with using keywords or hashtags related to books or reading. Then, you can either message people privately about your club or post general messages to your followers. Cities, towns, and even neighborhoods will often have social media groups where you can post to recruit members from your local area.

- Bookclubs.com[15] offers technology to create and manage book clubs that are in-person, virtual, or online.

- Apps that facilitate community connections and events, like Meetup[16], can be useful for finding members and organizing book club meetings. They may be especially helpful if you want to start a public club, where new members can simply show up.

- See if **your public library** or other community space has a bulletin board where you can put up flyers with information about your book club and contact information. Be detailed about what your club will look like so people can accurately judge whether it's right for them.

- Other public spaces, like **bookstores and coffee shops**, also often have bulletin boards or designated areas where you can leave flyers. Make sure to ask for permission first, and try to target places you think readers who are good matches for your club might frequent.

No matter how you choose to recruit members, it's best practice to include as much information about your book group as possible so that prospective members will know whether or not the club will be right for them. Using the questions provided above, you can decide which aspects of your book group you want to be predetermined (for example, which genres you'll discuss, or how often you'll meet), and which you'll align on with your members at your first meeting.

What to Consider When Joining an Existing Book Club

If you're not looking to start a club yourself but to join one, a good place to begin is asking friends if they're already part of a group. If they say that they are but it's not open to new members, remember that this is most likely nothing personal, as one of the important dynamics of a book club is its size and many groups restrict their membership numbers. As already noted, many bookstores and libraries host book clubs and might also know of other local clubs. There's no one-stop resource that we know of for finding local groups, but with a little search engine legwork it's likely you'll have no problem — especially if you live in an urban area. For example, a quick search using the terms "book club new york" produces a wealth of potential options.

About one in five book club members belong to an online group. If you don't find a group to join locally, are interested in discussing a specific type of book, are too busy to join an in-person group, or just don't want the commitment — **you're almost certain to find a group online that's just what you're looking for.** Some online groups meet in real time, but most are run as online forums enabling people to participate when convenient. For example, BookBrowse hosts discussions at bookbrowse.com/onlinebookclub[17], and you're very welcome to join us!

Common Concerns When Starting a Book Club

What if you do want to start your own club but aren't exactly feeling confident? Maybe you're not a particularly extroverted person or someone who typically brings others together, or you don't feel your organizational skills are the best. You *want* a book club to happen, and maybe can even envision what you want it to look like, but are doubtful about making it a reality. The good news is that it's normal to feel this way before undertaking any big venture, and no matter who you are, you can approach this project thoughtfully and play to your strengths. Below, we look at a few common concerns and how to address them.

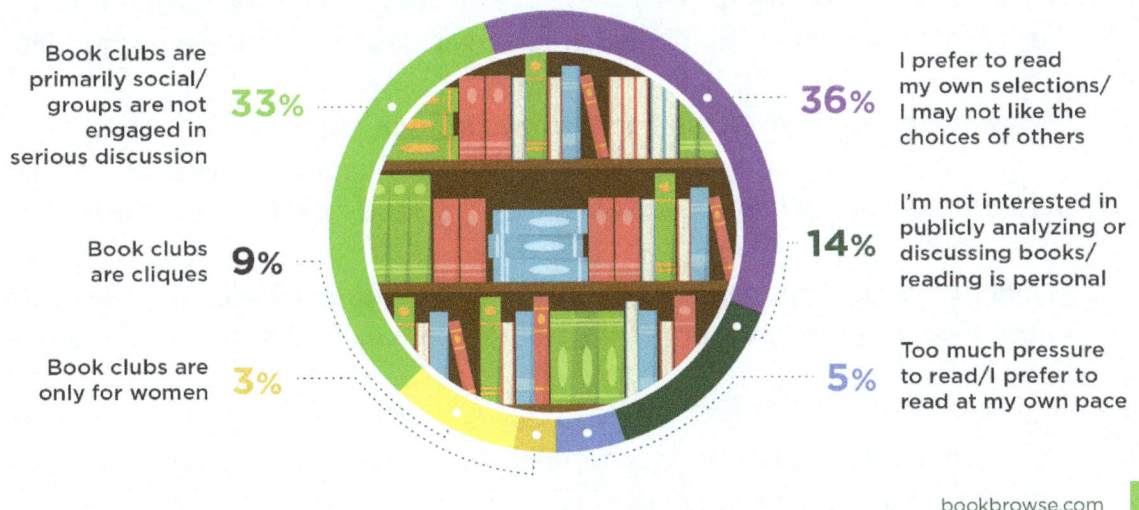

Primary reason for not being interested in a book club

- Book clubs are primarily social/groups are not engaged in serious discussion — 33%
- Book clubs are cliques — 9%
- Book clubs are only for women — 3%
- I prefer to read my own selections/I may not like the choices of others — 36%
- I'm not interested in publicly analyzing or discussing books/reading is personal — 14%
- Too much pressure to read/I prefer to read at my own pace — 5%

bookbrowse.com

"I'm shy/introverted. How can I lead a book group or get one together?"

For one thing, just because you decide to start a club doesn't mean you have to be the group's sole leader or discussion facilitator. Many groups trade off on this task, and you may find it easier to manage after watching someone else do it. If you feel intimidated by leading a group or the prospect of reaching out to people to start a club, try teaming up with one or two friends to share the load. This way, you can play to your strengths and familiarities, at least initially. For example, maybe you feel relatively comfortable reaching out to people by email, but would prefer not to have to do too much solo talking at the first meeting.

"What if no one shows up or reads the book?"

While this is a legitimate and understandable concern to have, you can make it much less likely by being intentional about the kind of club you want to have and the people you want to connect with. By thinking and talking to others ahead of time about your vision for the book club, and by inviting others into the process of forming the club (through answering the questions in the last section, for example), you'll feel supported and confident that this is something you're all doing together.

"My ideal book club doesn't look like the kind of book club I'm used to seeing or hearing about. What if I can't find the right people for it/make it work?"

We found that many people have negative perceptions of book clubs. For example, that clubs are cliquey or full of drama, that there are no clubs for the particular types of books they're interested in, or that book clubs only cater to certain demographics.

> *"From what I've heard from friends (and seen in the media), book clubs often seem more about getting together and drinking wine and gossiping than actually discussing books."* — Female, 25-34, reads 5-6 books/month

> *"They are often monopolized by dominant individuals trying to impose their opinions and impress other members."* — Female, aged 55-64, reads about 1 book/month

> *"A bunch of white soccer moms gather in a crowded room borrowed from their church to discuss a boring book they all hate but they go anyways because it's something to keep them busy."* — Female, aged 18-24, reads about 1 book/month

No one is wrong in their feelings and fears about book clubs or what they've observed. The stereotype of book clubs generally being for groups of middle-aged women who are there ostensibly to read literary fiction but mostly to drink wine and go off-topic may make some people feel excluded by the culture or intimidated (or just uninterested) and others offended — because what's the problem with getting distracted by a little wine and gossip if everyone's into it? Nothing at all, and book clubs don't have to adhere to any particular formula, either, regardless of what you've seen before.

It may be that the idea of a book club you're familiar with doesn't mesh with what you want, and that's all the more reason to start your own. It may not be obvious, but there are very likely other people out there who are interested in your ideal group, even if you have to search them out online and/or make your club virtual. Start with what you're looking for, and think about what spaces your ideal members are already in — these are the spaces where you can begin to meet people who might be interested in joining your club.

Qualities of a Good Book Club Leader or Participant

Hopefully by now you have some idea of how you can begin to start or find your ideal book club, but what qualities should you endeavor to bring to your meetings? Whether you're starting your own book group or joining one as a new member, how can you be considerate of others and contribute to a fun and comfortable atmosphere? We'll cover more conversational specifics in the next chapter, but here are just a few basics to keep in mind.

Pay attention and be accommodating. A lot of being a good leader or member is sensitivity to what's happening around you. Whether you're facilitating a discussion or just participating, do what you can to ensure that everyone gets a chance to speak. If you've been talking for a while, ask if anyone else would like to contribute to the conversation. If someone else has been speaking on one subject for a long time or the conversation is lagging, see if you can redirect it.

Do your part. Whether you're the leader or a participant, do your best to hold up your end and do whatever you've agreed to — whether it's reading the book, showing up on time, bringing refreshments, or having a discussion guide on hand. The more everyone sticks to their assigned roles and contributions, the smoother discussions and all other aspects of the book club will run.

Get organized. Staying on task might not seem very fun, and if your club is more casual, it may be less necessary to think about. But it can be helpful to consider organization part of what *makes* a discussion fun. If you're leading the discussion, you can enjoy brainstorming the topics you want to introduce and anticipate hearing what other people have to say about them. If you're just participating, you can note things down you want to talk about as you read the book so you don't miss out on conversations you want to have! This can be a good strategy for keeping social anxiety at bay, too.

> *"I am introverted and do have social anxiety which can then become social awkwardness as I 'nervous talk'...I prepare notes beforehand with the things from the book I hope we talk about, or information I have researched in support of the author or book." — Jennifer*

This section has almost certainly given you a lot to think about, and you may even be feeling a bit intimidated. Remember that the above is meant to guide you, not to complicate the process. Some factors or considerations may not apply to the club you want, and if you already have people in mind to be in your club, a good first step may be getting together as a group to talk things out. A book club can benefit from a strong vision, but also from collaboration to lighten the load.

In the next section, we'll explore how to get your book club up and running, and how to keep it going strong!

Chapter 2: How to Run a Book Club Smoothly

Set Clear Expectations

One of the first and most important things you can do to ensure smooth sailing for your book club is to establish how it will be run and why.

Often, book club issues arise because members have not discussed and agreed upon the basic expectations of their group. For example, it will be difficult to have a harmonious get-together if some members think of meetings as an excuse for a fun night of catching up on local gossip with a few minutes spent on the book if time allows, while others anticipate an in-depth discussion of the book. Both are valid ways to run a book club, they're just not compatible expectations for members in the same group. **Discussing and agreeing on the core objectives of the group will help prevent problems from happening, and make resolving them easier if they do.** A simple set of guidelines, made together, can work wonders.

Specifics to discuss when drawing up guidelines could include our "Questions to Answer When Starting a Book Club" earlier in this book. Here are a couple of broader considerations that may also help you align your expectations:

- **Your goals.** For example, do you all ultimately want to get to know each other better through book discussions? To explore challenging, in-depth questions? Or to just have fun? Understanding what you want in your book club will affect (and help direct) the books you choose, how discussions are handled, and how you use your time.

- **Your values.** In conjunction with the types of goals mentioned above, what deeper personal reasons and motivations lie behind individual desires to read and connect over books? Do some of you want to discover and make a point of supporting new and less established authors? Are some seeking insight into a certain aspect of your (perhaps shared) identity? Do other members want to have a better overall understanding or appreciation of literature? Or is your club made up of a group of friends who feel making time for each other is most important, while the books are secondary?

The group doesn't need to have all the same values or even all the same goals, but goals and values should be compatible. For example, one group member may be interested in exploring marginalized authors to gain insight into important work that struggles to get mainstream visibility. A member of that same group may want to read work by queer Black authors because they share that identity and feel it's a way of learning more about a community they belong to. These two people likely share some values and can probably agree on books they want to read, even while approaching those books for different primary reasons. They also both probably want to dedicate a substantial amount of meeting time to serious discussion. Understanding these types of differences and similarities can help you align expectations for what your group will look like and how it will run.

Prioritize Direct Communication

Even in the strongest book clubs, issues or tensions are likely to emerge at some point. We've found that it is how your group deals with these issues that's a key factor in long-term happiness.

In BookBrowse's research, we've seen that when problems arise some people understandably choose not to address them directly and instead look the other way. After all, book clubs are often comprised of friends, neighbors, or co-workers, so a confrontational situation could potentially affect other aspects of members' lives. But while sometimes problems resolve themselves, they often do not. The tension that builds around unresolved issues can fester and lead to members leaving the group or, worse, the dissolution of the book club. This is why it's important to facilitate and encourage direct communication between members.

Set aside time regularly for the group to discuss how things are running, and provide a forum for raising issues and new ideas.

This is important even when things seem to be going smoothly within a well-established group! The purpose of regularly carving out time to discuss how things are going is not to create change for change's sake, but to give people the opportunity to share ideas about what's working well and what might be improved.

Interestingly, in our research, we saw that among those who left a previous book club due to dissatisfaction, 62% stayed with the group for more than a year, and 37% stayed for more than three years. It makes us wonder how many of these people might still have been in their book club if there had been a regular forum for discussing issues. One person shared their book club's process for checking in with members: "We have a planning meeting in January of each new year to discuss how we all feel about how we structure our meetings. We also exchange ideas on how to improve our get-togethers."

The Book Club Health Check

When evaluating the overall happiness and health of your book club, it can help to be aware of specifics like the interpersonal dynamics, the level of organization, and the quality of discussions. With these factors in mind, there are things your club can do to proactively manage conflict, or even prevent issues from arising in the first place. Just like an annual checkup at the doctor can help spot problems with your physical health before they become serious, an annual book club "health check" can help prevent a group from stagnating or unexpressed tensions reaching a breaking point.

Here's a list of possible questions, both logistical and interpersonal, to consider discussing and answering with your group. It's best to keep the opening questions broad so the discussion can flow in the direction most relevant to your club. The notes under each topic heading aren't intended to be an exhaustive list of questions to ask, but rather possible discussion prompts if you feel the conversation needs direction.

To make it easier for you to conduct a Book Club Health Check, we've also created a survey template which you can modify. The template is included at the end of this book and is also available at bookbrowse.com/bchc[18].

What's the first word you would use to describe your group?

This can be useful as a quick calibration of the group's feelings and as an icebreaker to give everyone a chance to speak.

Are the meeting frequency, time, and location(s) working well for everyone?

Most groups meet monthly but some find it better to meet more or less frequently, or skip certain times of the year.

Are there any issues to discuss relating to attendance and reading the book?

Topics that might come up or that could be introduced include:

- Is it okay to frequently skip meetings?

- If somebody is going to miss a meeting, do they need to let the group know? If so, how?

- Is it okay to come to the meeting without having read the book? If yes, is it fair to ask others not to discuss spoilers?

Is everyone happy about the types of books being discussed and the process for selecting them?

Possible topics:

- Is the process of selecting books working for everyone? If not, how can it be improved?

- How far ahead of time should the group be picking books?

- Are the books that are being chosen sufficiently challenging/interesting?

- Are there different genres or types of books people would like to be reading?

- Are the voices of everyone who wants to be involved in the selection process being heard?

Is the size of the group working well?

Possible topics:

- If the group is relatively small, would members like to grow the group? If so, how do you want to go about finding new members?

- If the group is large, would people like to consider breaking into separate groups for discussions?

- What should the current policy be on new members? Can people just bring friends with them or do they have to check with the group first? Do new members have to be approved by all/some of the group?

Is there a good balance between discussion time and social aspects?

Possible topics:

- Is the amount of time spent discussing the book working for everyone? Would people like to spend more or less time on discussion? (Most people we surveyed who were dissatisfied with their group said they would like more — and more focused — discussion time, not less.)

- If the group isn't getting as much time to discuss the book as they would like, how can meetings be restructured to allow for this?

- Is the level of hosting asked of members (including food) fun or stressful?

What about the discussions themselves?

Possible topics:

- Are meetings structured so that everyone interested in contributing feels they have enough of an opportunity to speak? If not, how could you improve this?

- Is it okay to go off-topic, and what does the group consider "off-topic" in relation to a book? What about side discussions?

- If the group has trouble staying on topic, what can be done to respectfully steer the conversation back to the book? (According to our research, about three-quarters of groups designate someone to facilitate the discussion, often rotating the role.)

- Would people be interested in varying the discussion format? For example, every now and then, instead of just discussing a single book, you could separately read different books on a particular topic and discuss them, or watch a movie adaptation of a book and compare the two.

Is the group's overall organization and communication working well?

Possible topics:

- Does anyone feel they are carrying too much of the organizational load or, conversely, would like to be more involved (e.g., organizing meetings, finding book club resources, hosting duties)?

- Are communications sent between meetings effective?

- If a member consistently breaks the group's rules and/or is disruptive, how will this be handled?

- Does anyone feel that the group could better support their individual needs or concerns? (For example, regarding issues like transportation/accessibility around meetings, financial costs associated with the book club, discussion topics that are more personal/political for some than others, etc.)

Is there anything not already covered that members of the group would like to start or stop doing?

For example, some groups like to organize special events like themed dinners related to a book, or invite authors to meetings. Others enjoy going to author readings, getting involved in work that serves the community, or going on trips together. Conversely, some groups may feel that they are doing too much and would like to cut back to the basics of book discussion.

Next steps

Having taken the time to discuss these issues, make sure to agree on what (if any) changes your group is going to make, and make note of any key points for future reference.

Remember, book clubs are as diverse as book club members. To find the best way to manage your unique group, communicate honestly with one another and be willing to listen and work together to find the best solution when problems arise. Just as there is no single right way for a book club to run, there is no one right way to resolve book club issues. But fostering a mutually supportive atmosphere where members have clear opportunities to ask for their needs and preferences to be accommodated will probably make people less likely to leave the group.

If your book club cultivates an environment of open honesty, non-judgment, and accountability—a place where people respectfully listen to one another and also take responsibility for how their words affect others—**discussing these topics as a group should provide real opportunities for growth and long-term book club health.** In the next chapter, we'll look at how to foster a similarly supportive atmosphere in your book discussions.

Chapter 3: Choosing and Sourcing Books

How to Choose Books

A lot of books are enjoyable to read but don't contain much to discuss, while others are hard-going but generate great discussions. The sweet spot for book clubs, of course, is books that are enjoyable *and* good for conversation. One way to increase the chances of reading this kind of book is to make it a requirement for the person choosing or recommending a book for your club to have read it first. (The possible exception to this being books already established as book club favorites.)

What exactly makes a book a good one for discussion largely depends on the group discussing it, of course. Members we surveyed suggested they prioritize a book being well-written, challenging, and inspiring. They also consider whether a book is topical and whether it has been successful with other clubs, among other factors.

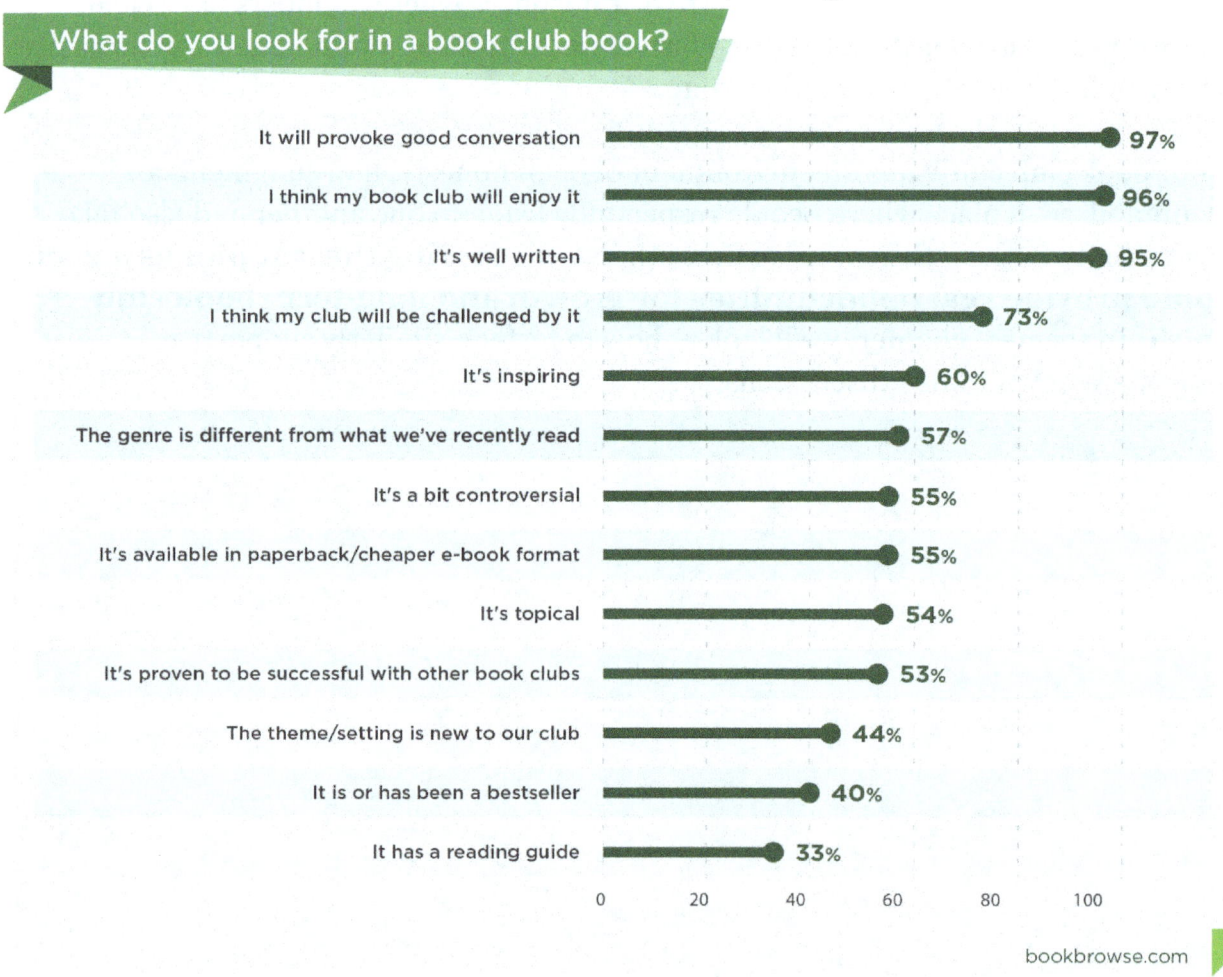

There are many different ways to choose books for your book club, and there's no reason to stick with the same formula all the time. Here are a few suggestions:

- **Let each person take a turn choosing a book** and, unless there's mass disagreement, their choice stands.

- **Have one person be responsible for bringing, say, three choices to a meeting** and let the group decide which one to read.

- **Have everyone bring a suggestion** and agree on the top choices to read — and then the next few months of books are decided.

- **Use BookBrowse!** We only feature books we wholeheartedly stand behind, and have a section of recommended book club reads — including our Top 10 Book Club Recommendations[19] list of most-viewed book club titles, updated weekly.

- **Choose a theme for two to three books in a row.** Or revisit the same theme from time to time. (For example, some clubs make a point of reading a book set locally or by a local author at least once a year.) BookBrowse's book club recommendations are sorted by title, author, genre, time period, setting, and theme.

- **Look for recommendations at your local library or bookstore.** Most libraries have lists of recommended titles and "librarian picks," and many will be happy to work with you and your group to find book choices you're likely to enjoy. Some even have special book club kits you can borrow with multiple copies of the book, or will help source copies within the library's collection.

- **Check out lists of books that have won awards**, like the Pulitzer, Booker, and National Book Award. Many of these books make good choices for book clubs. Visit the Award Winners[20] section of the BookBrowse website for inspiration.

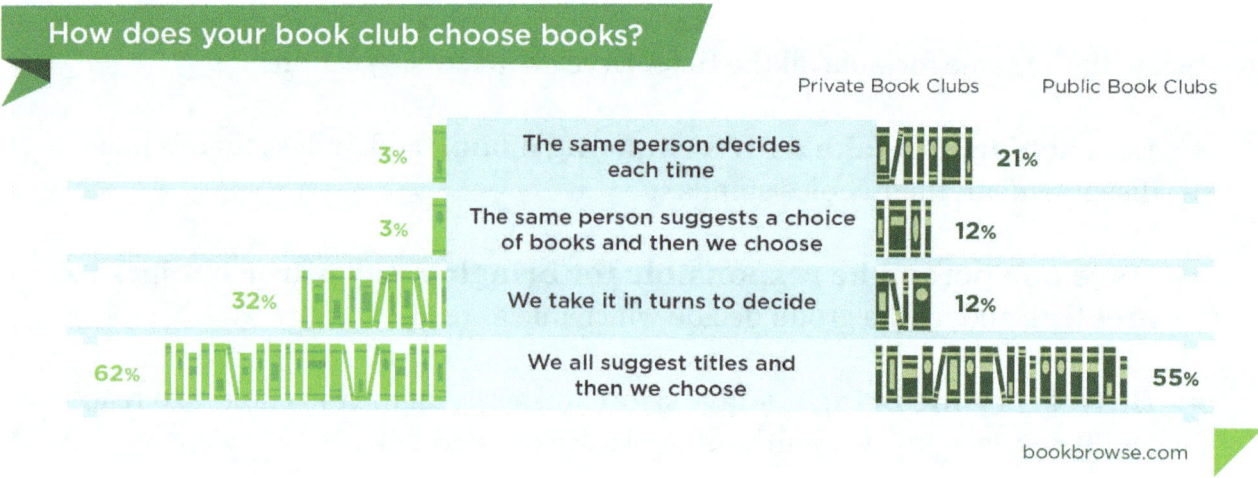

Regardless of how you decide to choose books, here are some additional considerations you may find helpful:

- It's unlikely that everybody will agree on every book choice every time. **Consider deciding that a majority vote will carry.** Also, encourage members to treat new genres or authors with an open mind — after all, most people join a book club at least in part to expand their reading experience.

- **Select your books at least two meetings ahead**, so you have time to buy/borrow and read the book. Some groups plan their entire year's reading at one meeting, others prefer to stay just a few books ahead (40% of groups plan at least four months ahead).

- However, **be cautious of committing to books *too* far ahead** as the mood and interests of the group will likely change over time, and you could find yourselves tied to a book that people aren't excited to read anymore.

- **Avoid getting stuck in a rut.** If the last few books have been contemporary fiction, how about a nonfiction title? If you've been reading a lot of historical fiction, how about a fantasy? Some genres and subgenres might produce more books suitable for discussion than others, but every genre has books that are good for book clubs.

- **If your club is based on a particular theme or angle, discuss how you want to see it reflected in your book choices**, as this may not be obvious. For example, if a group's shared goal is to read more about the environment and climate change, some members may assume they'll be reading contemporary nonfiction, while others may see literary fiction, science fiction, history, and other genres as being plenty relevant to the subject.

- **Early on, avoid books that seem likely to create controversy or difficult discussion.** What these are will depend largely on the makeup of your book club, and the best way to avoid unproductive discomfort or a hostile environment is to put some thought towards verifying member compatibility in the first place. But your initial meetings may go more smoothly if you don't try to tackle topics that are too intellectually or emotionally taxing for members right away.

- In a similar vein, at least **for the first few meetings, choose reasonably short books** with an already prepared reading guide.

A discussion guide, also known as a reading guide, is simply a list of questions or suggested topics. Not only can the discussion guide provide interesting avenues for conversation, but the existence of one signals that the book is likely a good choice for book clubs.

Don't feel you have to follow the guide rigidly (and don't read it until you've read the book, as it will likely have spoilers), it's simply a resource to get the conversation going and to turn to if the discussion is running out of steam or going off course.

BookBrowse's book club recommendations all come with reading guides, most of which you can access right on the site.

In an upcoming section, we'll go into more detail about discussion guides, including how to create your own! But first, let's look at how to get your hands on the books you want to read.

Buying or Borrowing — and Alternatives!

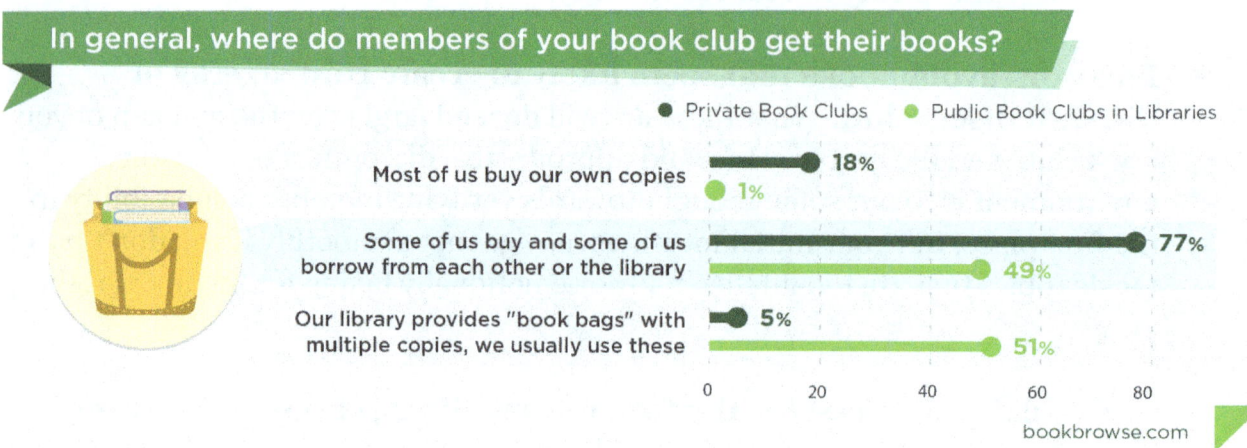

If your book club can support local libraries and indie bookstores, this is a great thing to do. And keep in mind that resources like Libby[21] (a library app) and Bookshop.org[22] (a site where you can buy books online from local stores) make it possible to do so from a distance. You'll be contributing to the continuation of a literary ecosystem that benefits readers, writers, workers in the book business, and other book clubs everywhere. Buying used books locally, if you can, is a way of supporting your community while still saving a few dollars.

Additionally, libraries often offer book club kits, or sets of multiple copies of a certain book intended specifically for book clubs. The kits may include extras like a reading guide or other resources for enhancing your discussions. Even if your local library doesn't currently have book club kits, you can let them know you would be interested, and they may end up carrying them in the future.

But what if buying books (or particular books) isn't an option for some members, or if you're limited in the library resources available to you individually or as a group? A common challenge to starting a book club is a lack of accessibility. This can apply to spaces (someone may be unable to attend physical meetings due to a lack of accommodation for chronic illness or disability) but also materials — someone may not be able to provide books for themselves or a group through buying or borrowing.

Depending on where your members live and how flexible they can be, sharing copies of a book (whether purchased or from a library) may be an option. In our research, we've found that many book club members are comfortable sharing books, and this can save considerably on time and money.

There are also many places online where you can find **books that are out of copyright and legally free to download**, like Project Gutenberg[23]. If you're looking for more contemporary books, then BookBub[24] is a good source for free or substantially discounted ebooks.

If you don't have an e-reading device, though, reading whole ebooks can be annoying, and there are sometimes logistical hurdles when it comes to downloading. In this case, another option to consider is **online short stories**. Even people not normally comfortable reading on a screen might feel up to one or two stories, and there are many available from older collections.

For contemporary stories, **online literary magazines** frequently offer some free access to issues, and can be a fantastic resource for discovering new authors before their books hit the shelves. The *Poets & Writers* website has a search tool for finding lit mags[25] that match your genre specifications. (This is intended for writers looking to submit their work, but is a useful way for readers to see what's currently out there, too.)

You can also find **free audiobooks** of varying lengths on Project Gutenberg or dedicated sites like LibriVox[26].

Chapter 4: Preparing for and Having Successful Discussions

Creating and Sourcing Book Club Questions

Many books already have matching reading guides (also known as discussion guides, or just book club questions) produced by the publisher. These guides can often be found at the back of the book or on the publisher's website. **At BookBrowse, we make it easy for you to track down titles accompanied by book club questions.** Anyone can check out our extensive selection of reading guides[27] under the "Book Clubs" menu on the homepage, and use this feature to align their book club selections with pre-written discussion questions.

But many books that are worthwhile for book clubs don't have a published discussion guide or book club questions available. In this situation, you have a couple of options. If you'd like to have a more structured, specific reading guide on hand, you can create your own! If you aren't so concerned about keeping things structured or prefer a simpler, low-effort option, some all-purpose questions get the job done. We'll look into the details of both of these approaches below.

Writing Discussion Questions Yourself

First, your DIY guide will be easier to produce if you **take notes as you read**, rather than relying on your memory to zero in on topics after the fact.

As you're putting your guide together, keep in mind that your goal is to foster a positive atmosphere for conversation. You therefore want to **avoid questions that people can respond to in just a word or two**, such as simple yes/no questions.

> Weak: Did you like the book?

> Better: What did you like about the book?

You also don't want to bore people or make them feel like they're taking a test! To this end, **stay away from questions that seem to suggest correct or incorrect answers**:

> Avoid: In what year did John Doe commit treason?

Weak: Describe the protagonist's primary motivation for committing treason.

Better: Why do you think John Doe committed treason?

Note that the better question above is personal; **using "you" invites participants to express their opinions**.

For an even more effective question, **pull the reader's emotions and imagination into the discussion**:

Better still: Why do you think John Doe committed treason? Did you approve of his actions? What would you have done in his shoes?

Another way to draw people into conversation is to **invite them to compare their experiences of a time, setting, or event to how it's portrayed in the book**:

What do you remember about the 1960s? Did the author's portrayal of the time period align with your recollections?

Have you ever been to Appalachia? What did you think of the author's descriptions of the area?

Have you ever tried or wanted to try backpacking? Did the author make it seem more or less appealing to you than before reading the book?

Asking questions about specific experiences may be most appropriate if you're facilitating a discussion for your own book club. For example, if everyone in your group has lived through the '60s, the above question about that era makes perfect sense, but you may want to phrase the question differently depending on your club's make-up.

Something else that's important when it comes to identities and experiences is to generally **avoid assumptions about people** who may be responding to your questions, and **avoid questions that position any person or people as the subject of a debate**.

Not keeping these things in mind may (however unintentionally) alienate people with a personal stake in a topic and put them in the position of watching others discuss their realities in a casual and theoretical way. Instead, **aim your questions towards everyone while also showing deference to those who are closest to a subject**:

Avoid: Have you ever met any undocumented migrants like those in the story? What do you think our government should do about immigration?

> Better: What do you think the author means to convey about the reality of living as an undocumented person? What problems with the current immigration system do the characters' experiences expose?

Note how the second example asks questions in a way that doesn't assume participants' identities (citizenship status or history, in this case) and doesn't suggest that anyone's existence may be invalid or itself a topic of discussion open to debate. It also centers the experience that's being discussed from the point of view of those having that experience within the context of the book.

While book clubs should definitely be a place to share opinions and benefit from the opinions of others, not everyone is on equal ground with all subjects, and not everyone speaks from the same set of experiences, and how opinions are informed by facts and experience matters. Bearing this in mind will help provide direction and accountability for a productive discussion.

Many readers like to share passages or quotes from the book, so **including a question that prompts people to mention their favorite parts** can be helpful and spark further conversation:

> Is there a specific quote or passage in the book that spoke to you? What about it stood out, and why do you feel it resonated with you?

And **providing a specific quote to discuss** can be even better, as it gives people a question unique to the book:

> Oran tells Sarah that "Grief is a dark labyrinth." What do you suppose he means? Do you agree?

Using Generative AI to Create Discussion Questions

Tools like ChatGPT [28] offer the opportunity to quickly generate book club questions. Ethical considerations of using these tools aside, there are practical issues as well. The more recently the book has been published, the less data about the title the tool will have access to - even using AI mode on Google to look through the most recent data may result in inaccurate or surface level questions (or a rehashing of book club questions already available on the web).

If you do decide to use AI, it's best to provide it with your own notes (see sample note prompts in the back of the book) in order to provide the tool with more unique 'context'. The more instructions you provide, the better the questions will be.

You will also need to double check the accuracy of the questions as well. We understand that coming up with discussion questions may seem daunting at first, which is why the allure of a tool that will generate them for you is enticing, but you may find that with practice it's actually easier for you to write the questions yourself than it is to use generative AI, particularly for more recently released titles.

Book Club Discussion Questions for Any Book!

If you don't feel you need a book-specific discussion guide, check out some all-purpose discussion questions that you can use for *any* book below. Simply pick one to three topics from most of the categories for a well-rounded discussion.

General Book Club Questions

- What did you like best/least about the book, and why?
- Did you have expectations of the book (e.g., from reading reviews, hearing from friends)? If so, did it fall short, meet expectations, or exceed them?
- What do you think of the book title and jacket cover? Do you think they adequately reflect the book's content, or are they misleading? If you had creative control, what changes would you make, if any?
- Are you glad you read the book?
- What did you learn from the book? Did it change your perception? Did it leave you with questions you want to find answers to?
- Do you have a favorite quote or scene from the book? Why does this stand out to you?
- How do you think the book will age (or has aged)? If the book is recently published: Do you think it is one that people will still be reading in decades to come? If it was published in the past: Is it still relevant? If it was written now, how would it be different?
- Have you read other books on the same topic? If so, which would you recommend?
- What did you think of the book's ending?
- What audience would you recommend the book to?
- If you were making a movie of the book, who would you cast?

Book Club Questions About the Author or Their Writing

- Why do you think the author chose to write this particular book? What are they trying to convey, and are they successful in doing so?
- How would you describe the author's writing style? What did you like or not like about it?

- Does the author's writing style remind you of any other authors? If so, in what ways?
- If you were writing this book, would you tell the story the same way?
- If you could ask the author one question, what would it be?

Book Club Questions Focused on the Book's Story

- Was the story credible? For example, even in a fantasy setting, the characters' motives and actions need to make sense within the context of their world.
- What did you think of the pacing of the book? Did it hold your interest throughout? Were some parts too fast or slow?
- Did the author use symbolism? If so, what was the purpose of the symbolism? What was the author trying to convey?
- Did the plot proceed as you expected? What parts of it surprised you, if any?
- Did you wholly trust the narrator(s), or did you consider them unreliable in any way?

Book Club Questions About the Book's Characters

- Did you relate to a particular character or the circumstances they were in?
- Which character would you most like to meet? Why?
- How does the person (or people) who relate(s) the story color the telling?
- If the story had been told from a different perspective, what would have been different? Would you have liked to hear from another character?
- Are the characters believable? For example, does a child narrator sound the age they are? Does the voice of a character in a historical novel seem true to the period? Do you think it's meant to?
- If you were the main character, would you have acted as they did?
- What do you imagine might happen to the characters after the story ends?

Book Club Questions for the Book's Setting

- How well did the author paint a picture of the setting?
- How did the setting impact the story? If the setting had been different, would the story have been different?
- Would you like to visit the setting of the book? If familiar with the setting, did it ring true?

Genre-Specific Book Club Questions

Nonfiction: Was the author able to convey things in an enjoyable way for a non-expert reader? Do you feel the author justified their conclusions? Do you feel the author provided an appropriate amount of information for the text?

Memoir: Were there gaps in the story you wish had been filled, or parts where you wished for less information? (If the book is fiction with biographical elements, why do you think the author chose to write the story in this way rather than as a memoir?)

Short Stories: Which story did you like best/least, and why? How are the stories connected? For example, what settings, themes, or characters do they share? Would you have liked to see any of these stories extended?

Historical Fiction: Do you feel the book was well-researched? Did you spot any anachronisms, or any period-specific aspect that wasn't mentioned but that you feel should have been?

Mysteries: When did you figure out "whodunnit"? What did you think of the red herrings the author inserted? Did you find them appropriate or forced? Was the ending satisfying?

General Book Club Topics Relating to the Book

Finally, you may want to include one or more general interest topics that relate to the book but don't require detailed knowledge of the text. These can be especially helpful if your book group has a relaxed policy about members attending meetings without having completed the book.

For example, these are some topics from past discussions on BookBrowse that relate to the book being discussed, but don't require a person to have read the book in order to participate:

- If you could start a movement in your community, what would it be? And why?
- Do you think it's true that we care less about others' opinions as we age?
- What are popular and favorite recipes of your family and region?
- Do you agree that "marriage is such a dreadful gamble"?
- Do you see the appeal of the [insert detail relevant to the book] lifestyle/career choice?

Preparing for Sensitive and Respectful Discussions

Over the years, BookBrowse has received many inquiries from book club members seeking guidance on how to navigate discussions around sensitive topics, particularly those related to race and social issues. As we note in our advice for writing discussion questions, book clubs provide a valuable space for members to share perspectives and learn from one another. However, it's also important to recognize that different lived experiences shape our understanding of these topics in meaningful ways. Some members of your book club may be able to speak to how certain issues impact their day-to-day lives, while other members' lives may be more removed from these issues, so it's important to acknowledge and consider this when sharing opinions. When discussing childbirth, for instance, many people would intuitively give more weight to the opinion of a mother who has gone through labor over that of a man who hasn't. In short, not everyone's opinions carry equal weight on all subjects.

Creating a thoughtful and respectful conversation means considering the broader context in which issues exist, no matter what your book group looks like. Not all forms of marginalization or inequality are visible, and not all perspectives about subjects like racism or prejudice are equally correct or respectful. Being mindful of this helps ensure that all members are respected and fosters more enriching and inclusive dialogue.

As already covered somewhat in our guide to writing discussion questions, showing this kind of mindfulness, as either a participant or moderator, can look something like the following:

- Insofar as it may not be obvious, **don't assume the identities of people in your discussion group, and be sensitive to the possibilities and probabilities of an author's intended audience.**

Take, for example, a novel by a Native author that includes expressions of Native language and culture. The book likely isn't written with the primary goal of making everything easy to understand for American readers outside of that culture. However, some readers might feel justified in criticizing it for not being more "accessible" to them. They may not realize that this expectation comes from a longstanding societal norm that assumes that books should be written for readers with a white American perspective.

Meanwhile, book club members who belong to marginalized groups may recognize that engaging in this kind of discussion would require them to explain or justify their own experiences — something that can be uncomfortable and exhausting. Rather than risk turning the conversation into a debate about their reality, they might simply decide to step away from the club altogether.

- **Defer to the opinions of those with expertise or experience on a particular topic.** In other words, assume that marginalized people are experts on their own lives. This can apply to how participants speak to other participants but also how people might speak about characters and authors. Additionally, don't create or allow debates that question the validity of any person or group's identity, existence, or well-being. (See the immigration example in the Writing Discussion Questions Yourself section.)

- **At the same time, avoid singling out visible minorities in the group or expressing the expectation for a marginalized person to educate others.** Instead, focus on creating an atmosphere where people with experience relatable to the subject at hand would feel safe and comfortable speaking about their personal experience if they chose to do so, and equally safe and comfortable not doing so.

For instance, the person in the example above could acknowledge that perhaps they are not the Native author's target audience and share with the group how they took responsibility for their reading experience by filling their knowledge gaps through research and context clues. This might inspire someone else in the group to share corresponding personal cultural knowledge, but without putting them in a position of obligation.

Your group can benefit from being mindful of the above both when having discussions and when setting general guidelines and expectations, as this will inform your understanding of how various rules apply and should be interpreted. As the Seal Press discussion guide for Ijeoma Oluo's *So You Want to Talk About Race* explains, "Abuse is never okay, but what is often called 'abuse' in heated discussions on race is often simply people of color expressing very justified emotions about living in a white supremacist society." Consider how you'll handle the realities of privilege and inequality in your group, and how these realities should apply to the guidelines you set for language and behavior.

Resources

Ijeoma Oluo's So You Want to Talk About Race[29], mentioned above, is a good general guide for having discussions about race, and is also a great book club pick in its own right for groups wanting to explore this subject. Its reading guide is intended for clubs discussing the book itself, but it opens with guidelines that can also be applied to book club discussions about race in general. These questions and guidelines are freely available on the publisher's page for the book as well as on the BookBrowse website[30].

Elaine Castillo's How to Read Now[31] is a lively book of essays exploring the ethics of reading. We recommend it to any clubs or members interested in getting into the nitty-gritty of how politics and privilege factor into how we experience books (and by extension, book discussion).

Why Appoint a Facilitator or Moderator?

Even if your members are used to being part of group discussions and listening to each other, it can still be a good idea to have somebody lead the meeting, in part to make sure that everyone's voices get heard, but also so that person can be prepared with thoughts on what topics to discuss. If there is a lag in conversation, the moderator can step in and suggest a new point or question for the group to consider.

The exact role of a moderator or facilitator will vary from group to group. Some book clubs might have a consistent moderator — for example, if your group is run by the local library, a librarian will probably lead the meetings. Some groups rotate the role, while others may not feel they need one at all. In general, we recommend having a moderator and rotating the role.

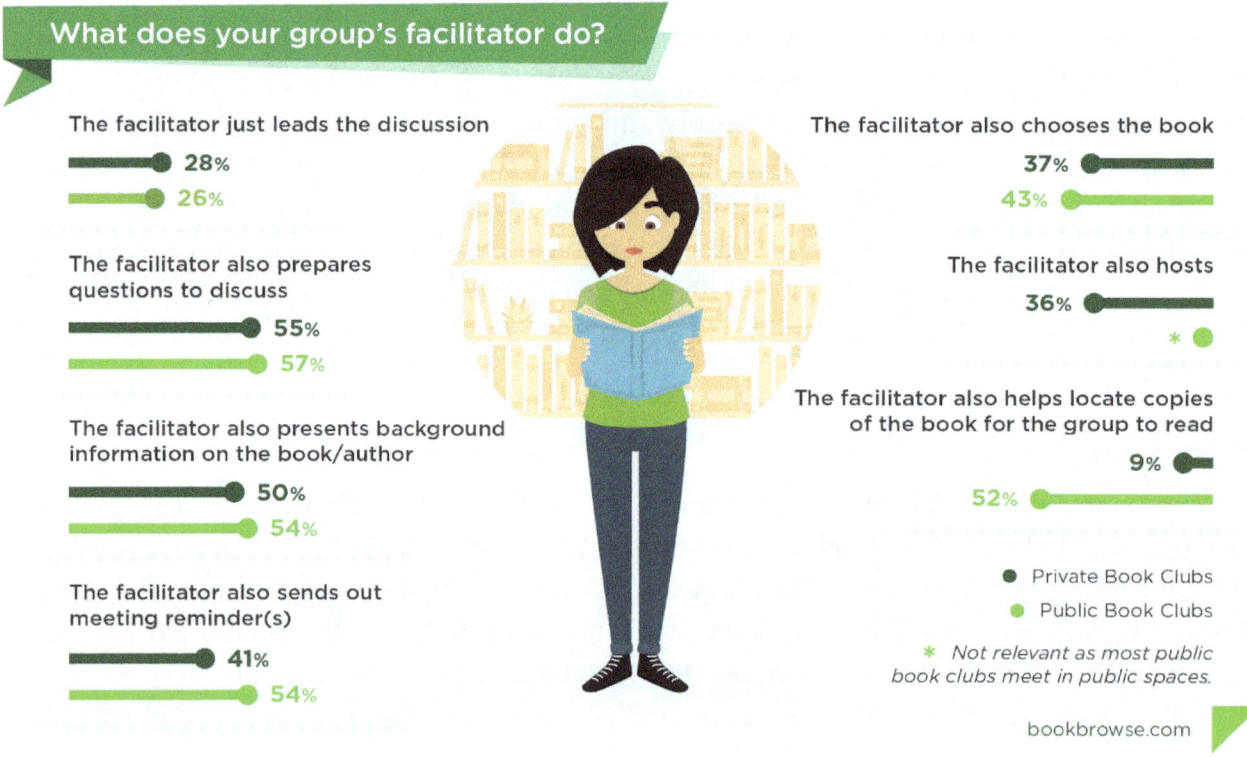

As the facilitator, your job is to:

- **Keep the meeting on track.** Digressions are fine but if the conversation strays too far off topic it's your job to bring it back.

- **Introduce new topics of discussion** if the conversation seems to be flagging.

- **Make sure everyone feels their voice has been heard** and that no one person's voice is heard too much. (And that includes your own!)

- **Keep things productive and respectful.** People may disagree, but as moderator, you can direct the conversation down constructive avenues and strive for accountability and respect in how participants treat each other and express themselves.

According to our research, **book clubs with facilitators report higher satisfaction with their overall experience:** 75% of those in facilitated groups reported feeling "very happy" in their book club, compared to 65% in groups that are not facilitated. Book clubs that do well without a facilitator tend to be either those that lean more towards being social groups, or ones where the membership have spent time establishing ground rules so that all participants feel confident redirecting the discussion when needed.

But even groups that do just fine without a facilitator in person might benefit from someone in the role when chatting virtually. For example, it's easier for people to accidentally talk over each other online, and a facilitator can be on the lookout for those who want to express their thoughts on a topic but haven't had a chance to speak. In some cases, the facilitator might ask each person if they want to share their thoughts on a topic before opening the discussion up to the group as a whole.

More than three-quarters of book clubs have a facilitator. Most groups rotate the role, but if somebody doesn't feel comfortable facilitating, there's no rule that says everyone has to take a turn.

Side note: Based on our research, facilitators frequently take on organizational duties, but be careful that the facilitator doesn't have to do too much! In some book clubs, particularly public groups such as those organized by libraries, we found that administration falls largely or completely on one person and that many leaders would like to see the load shared more equally (and conversely, some members of these groups would like to have a greater say in the club).

Facilitating a Discussion

Okay, it's your turn to moderate/lead your book club's discussion! What can you do to ensure a successful meeting? Below are some suggestions and tips.

Prepare discussion questions ahead of time. If you have a discussion guide, look through it before the discussion opens and decide which topics you think your group will find stimulating. Look for questions that make people think or draw out personal opinions, and generate good conversation (and remember, yes-or-no questions are a big snooze). If you choose to create the topics/questions yourself, jot down notes, poignant quotes, and page numbers while you read so they're handy for the meeting. Have a good topic ready to start the conversation and more ready to introduce if the discussion flags, goes off-topic, or starts to repeat itself. Your preparation will help keep the conversation on track and add depth to the discussion.

Consider doing some research ahead of the meeting. Background information on the book or author can deepen and enhance the reading and discussion experience. Find out what inspired an author to write a particular book, or learn more about the underlying history, culture, or context behind the book. Explore BookBrowse's author interviews and "beyond the book" articles, which provide digestible amounts of information that inform without overwhelming.

Send out reminders. Your group probably already has a fixed day and time to meet, but the location might change. Either way, a reminder of the time and location a few days ahead can be useful.

Once everyone is gathered, start with an organized approach. Remind the group when it's time for the discussion to start. If there are new members, make sure they are introduced. If there's any business to go over, like picking books for future meetings, you may want to cover these points before the discussion starts in case people need to leave quickly at the end.

If necessary, refresh people's memories on your group's ground rules — not all of them, just any where there have been issues. A minute or two on this can be time well spent. If you or other members feel there has been a problem in earlier meetings (e.g., one person dominating the conversation or too much off-topic conversation), this is the appropriate time to remind people what was previously agreed, and it may save you from having to confront someone during the meeting.

Consider asking all members to briefly give their opinion on the book. This ensures that everybody's voice is heard early on and also will give you a feel as to how the conversation will go, and what areas are most likely to be of interest. One book club member comments on the utility of this approach: "We start each meeting by going around the room asking what each person thinks of the book. This allows the quieter ones to have their say."

If the discussion takes on a life of its own, let it flow! It's quite likely that you won't get through all the potential topics you've thought of for discussion. In fact, after opening the discussion, you may not even need to introduce any. If the conversation is flowing well, it will naturally expand from the original topic into other interesting areas.

Don't be too rigid about keeping people on topic. As Harold Bloom (one of America's leading literary critics) said, the purpose of a book is "to get in very close to a reader and try to speak directly to what it is that they either might want out of the book or might be persuaded to see… [to persuade the reader] that certain truths about himself or herself, which are totally authentic, totally real, are being demonstrated to the reader for the very first time." In short, discussions do not have to stay rigidly about the book to be relevant. Many of the best discussions are triggered by the book and then the members discuss the topic from the perspectives of their own experiences.

Having said that, if the conversation is going way off-topic (which might be defined as the conversation not being of interest to the group as a whole), it's time to bring it back on track. Talking about personal experiences and how they relate to a particular book can enhance a group's discussion, but it can also be easy to get sidetracked. Before you know it, you're talking about a grandchild's choir concert or someone's yoga class, and the book discussion is lost in the mix, to the disappointment of some participants. In your role as facilitator, you should be recognized as an authority among friends and have the ability to bring the discussion back on track without being seen as "bossy," and this will probably be appreciated. As one book club member says, "Some people offer too much personal information that at the start relates to the book and then they get off track and others join them." Another comments, "There are always a couple of people who go a little too deep with their personal experience…It frustrates some of us."

Be ready to manage "overly dominant personalities." More than one-third of all book clubs report having an "overly dominant personality" — i.e., someone who, whether intentionally or not, talks too much and doesn't give others an equal opportunity to participate. As the facilitator, you can create the space needed for less assertive members to jump in. One facilitator says, "I carefully rein in the dominating ones while still allowing them to jump in. It is done delicately and sometimes with a bit of humor."

Warming Up to Discussion: Icebreakers

Regardless of how your club is structured and whether or not you appoint a facilitator, you may feel the need to break the ice a bit before you get down to discussing books. At your first meeting, or whenever new people join your reading group, it's nice to spend a bit of time getting to know each other. This can be as simple as going around the group and taking turns introducing yourselves, saying what you like to read, and what you're looking forward to about the book club (if you're new) or what you like about the club (if you're an established member).

But if this sounds a bit intimidating, or you just like the idea of getting to know people in a different way, an alternative is to play a game! The purpose of all the activities below is to give people a chance to meet each other and share information about themselves. Emphasize that (whatever activity you choose) it's meant to be a fun game, not a test, and that nobody will be keeping score.

Pass the Hat

This game is best in groups of about 10 people or less.

Think up one or more questions per person (if the group is large, have one question per person, if it's small then you might want to have two questions each). Cut the paper up so that each question is on its own piece, fold the papers, and put them in a container. Have each member pull out a question, then ask who would like to go first answering the question they drew (this avoids putting a person on the spot when they need a little time to think). Once somebody has answered their particular question, other participants might want to share their own answers. Keep an eye on the time and move on to the next question if things are going too slowly. If people are having trouble with the questions they were given, they could opt to swap with others.

Example Questions:
- What is the first book you remember reading/being read?
- What is your favorite book of all time?
- Which book has left the most lasting impression on you?
- Which book have you read most frequently?
- What books are on your bedside table at the moment?
- Name one book/author that you really can't stand.
- What type of books do you like reading most?

- If someone gave you money especially to buy a book, what book would you buy?
- Where's your favorite place to read?
- Which character in a book do you think is most like you?
- Which character in a book would you most like to be?
- What book do you plan to read next?
- Which literary character would you most like to have a "significant relationship" with?

Important: The questions above assume that the group members already consider themselves relatively well-read. If you're starting a group with people who may not think of themselves as "readers," it would be best to consider more generic questions, such as favorite sport, favorite place to visit, person you most admire, etc. This game is intended to help people feel comfortable with each other, not embarrass them!

Pair Share

If you think that some members of your group might feel uncomfortable coming up with a quick answer to a question in front of people they don't know well — as in Pass the Hat — arrange people in pairs (if there's one person left over, make a group of three) making sure that, whenever possible, each person is with somebody they don't know. Give each pair a short list of three to five questions and about ten minutes to "interview" each other. Have each person report back on what they found out about the other.

Wordplay

If you'd rather outsource the games to us, check out BookBrowse's latest Wordplay, which can always be found under the "Fun" menu on the homepage. This game, suggested by 91-year-old subscriber Antoinette Ciancarelli, involves guessing a common phrase or expression, and you can use it with your club or just for a bit of fun anytime!

One member says, "We play BookBrowse Wordplay at our book club at least once a month. I type out the 'expressions' on index cards and pass them around to the members to guess the meanings. I pass around a grab bag of inexpensive little gifts to the winners and tell them to close their eyes and pull out a gift."

Quiz

This works best for groups of eight or more. Give each person a copy of the quiz and a pencil, and about 15 minutes to find a person that fits each description, or knows the answer to the question. When time is up, reconvene the group and have fun sharing the answers.

These questions are ones that we thought up in a couple of minutes — you can probably come up with much better ones! Aim for about 10 to 20 questions. Use double-spacing so there's room to write down an answer.

For added fun, you could contact each person in advance and ask them for one interesting fact about themselves and include these in the quiz.

Example Quiz

Find somebody who:

1. Has read a book of poetry in the last year.
2. Likes to read in the bath.
3. Has fallen asleep with a book in their hands recently.
4. Reads more than one book at a time.
5. Likes to listen to audiobooks.
6. Has been in a book group before.
7. Has children.
8. Has been married for more than five years.
9. Will admit to being nervous being here.
10. Moved in the past two years.
11. Can quote at least two lines from Shakespeare.
12. Knows the heroine's name in *Wuthering Heights*.
13. Knows the name of one staff member at the local library.
14. Knows the name of Toni Morrison's first book.
15. Can recite a tongue twister.
16. Drives a red car.

Examples of questions specific to one group member. Obviously, you need to create questions relevant to your members...

17. Was born in South Africa.
18. Plays saxophone in a local band.
19. Has a dachshund named Lilly.
20. Favorite book of all time is *The Phantom Tollbooth*.

Chapter 5: Addressing Issues and Making Improvements

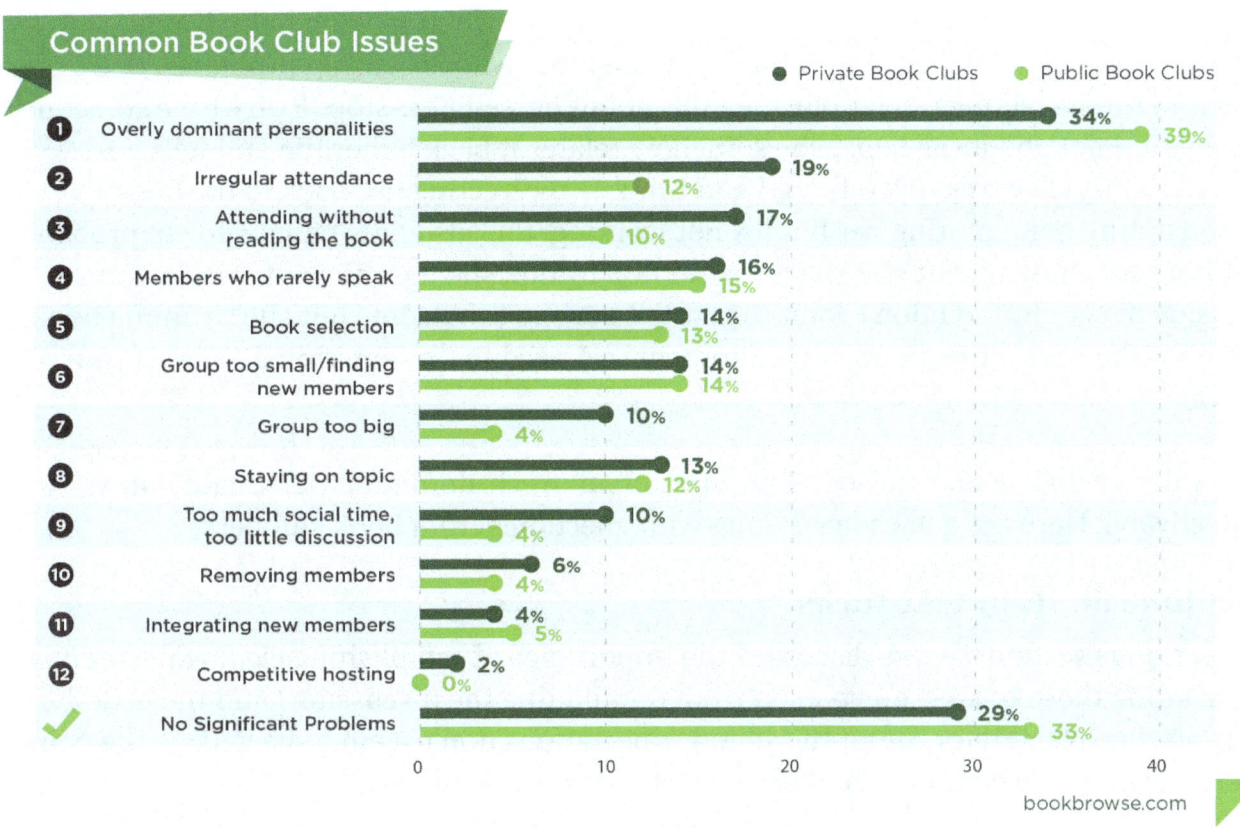

Keeping Discussions Focused

Our Preparing for and Having Successful Discussions chapter offers detailed advice on handling book club discussions from an in-depth perspective. But sometimes, even if you take the time to prepare for discussions and facilitate them perfectly, recurring issues with staying on topic or keeping the conversation balanced between participants still emerge. In cases like these, you may need to consider making a change. Read on for our suggestions on common discussion-related problems.

Dealing with Overly Dominant Personalities (ODPs)

In our research, we've found that one common cause of conflict in book clubs is overly dominant personalities (ODPs) — people who, whether intentionally or not, occupy too much of the limelight and overpower one or more elements of the book club, such as book selection or the discussion itself. Thirty-eight percent of those who left a book club due to dissatisfaction did so at least in part because of an overly dominant personality. ODPs can also worsen other common book club issues. For example, while 16% of all book clubs say that their group has been concerned about a member who rarely speaks, this figure rises to 26% in groups with an ODP.

One book club member gave us this real-life example when seeking help dealing with an ODP: "We recently gained a new book club member who is causing problems. She's only been to three meetings so far but she talks about herself non-stop. Every time someone makes a point about the book, she somehow relates it back to her life and tells a 10+ minute story. I've tried everything I can think — redirecting her back to the book, interrupting her, ignoring her but it's not working. She also puts people down, probably without meaning to, but still she does it. I don't think she has much of a social life outside of the club so I don't want to just tell her she can't come but she's ruining book club for the rest of the group at the moment so I need to do something. What is your advice?"

How does a book club resolve the problem of an overly dominant personality most effectively? Here are a few ideas, along with anecdotes from book clubbers.

Set time limits or take turns

In previous sections, we've discussed the importance of establishing clear expectations (including those to keep one person from dominating the discussion) and the benefits of appointing a facilitator. But if the stated expectations don't seem to be getting the point across, you may need to make those expectations more concrete.

Some groups **limit the amount of time or number of turns** each person has to express their opinions, sometimes using a physical prop as a reminder. One book club member says, "We ring a bell when someone goes on and on!" Another comments, "We give each person five note cards. A person has to throw a card into the hat each time she speaks." You can also simply designate a turn for each person to speak on a particular topic.

> "Most clubs I have been in go around in a circle so everyone gets to have time to contribute or pass." — Tamara VK

Communicate the problem to the group

If you don't feel it's necessary or productive to single out the offending person, first try communicating the problem of members dominating the conversation in general.

> "Send a general note or email to the whole group with guidelines for the meeting spelled out in black and white. You would not have to mention any

names, but just say that in the last few meetings the club has been straying and getting off topic." — Bridget G

Give the ODP a job to keep them focused

Some members suggest that it helps to encourage the ODP to contribute to the group in a different or additional way — for example, to take notes during the discussion or manage topics.

> *"We had a person like this in one of my book clubs. Totally unable to read social cues. You could avoid eye-contact, stop nodding, stop smiling, overtly look away, etc., and she wouldn't get it. We could've all passed out and fallen to the floor and she still would've continued her unrelated story. Interestingly, when she hosted a book, she was awesome...When she was in charge of keeping the questions going, she didn't have time to gallop away on a tangent."* — Coleen D

Communicate the problem to the ODP

Sometimes the overly dominant personality is unaware that they are causing an issue for the group, so a private conversation can help. A person can recognize that they talk more than others in their group without realizing it's a problem, and some book club members have reported that this approach was successful.

Discussions Straying Off-Topic

Sometimes, you may not have a problem with a particular person dominating the conversation but still find that it's hard to keep the group on topic. Almost every book club has times when the discussion veers off-topic. In most groups, such segues are either acceptable and/or the conversation is gently steered back to the book after a bit. But for some groups, it can become an issue.

About 13% of those in a book club say that their group has experienced differences of opinion about staying on topic when discussing books. Twenty-one percent of those who left a previous book club due to dissatisfaction cited off-topic discussion as a factor.

Sometimes problems are rooted in members having different definitions of what "off-topic" means. As with so many other book club issues, a good first step is for members to discuss and agree upon what the group as a whole considers a reasonable expectation. The best time to do this is not in the heat of the moment during a book discussion but at a separate time.

Side discussions and people talking over each other are frequent irritants, with many book club members finding them distracting and disrespectful. In our research, members stress the importance of ensuring all voices are heard. One facilitator says,

"The main problem we have is people talking among themselves about other things while we are having the book club discussion. We have had talks about this but it still happens...Since the group is large, sometimes several people speak at once. I have a little bell that I ring if too many are speaking at once."

Almost all book club members say it is okay to discuss personal experiences as they relate to the book, but toeing that fine line can be a challenge. This is why it's important to set clear expectations and, if necessary, make it someone's job to rein in the discussion when it strays too far from the book or topic at hand.

Regularizing Attendance

One email we received from a book club member asked for advice on an all too common book club problem. She wrote: "I started a book club about a year ago which has 14 members. We make book recommendations twice a year and then we vote on what books to read. It is expected that everyone rotate being a host and a discussion leader. One member has not attended a meeting for six months, and doesn't even RSVP to let us know that she won't be
attending (which we agreed was something we'd all do when we formed the group). I know she is not sick or traveling. Should I try to feel her out and ask if she wants to continue as a club member? Should our club care when members are no-shows and don't participate?"

We opened up this question to comments on social media and got many responses. More than three-quarters of those who commented felt that it was reasonable to expect book club members to make the book club a priority (including communicating if they cannot be at a meeting) — with a number stating that making an effort to attend is, simply put, the first rule of book club! Those in larger book clubs tend to be more relaxed on this point than smaller groups. Opinions were split on the right way to handle the situation, i.e., whether it was acceptable to just drop the member from the club mailing list, or whether the group should reach out to her directly to see what the problem is.

In general, book club members tend to emphasize **the importance of a consistent meeting day and time, and the value of good communication.** One notes, "We meet at the same time each month which has helped to solidify attendance. Communication is important, from a recap of meetings to reminders of upcoming meetings. A person in the club is great about emailing all of us the agreed-upon date and location for the next meeting."

When it's made clear that regular attendance or communication around attendance is required, it becomes easier to confront a member about irregular participation. Usually, this will either result in an improvement, or the member dropping out or being asked to leave. Furthermore, if you have a stated policy about what will happen when a member stops RSVPing or attending meetings, people will be more likely to follow it. Ultimately, it's easier to remove someone from a mailing list if they've already been told this is a possibility.

When People Don't Read the Books

Seventeen percent of those in private book clubs and 10% of those in public groups say their group has experienced problems with members who come to meetings without having finished the book (or, in some cases, without even starting it). In smaller groups, this can be an issue if there are insufficient members to hold a good discussion. One of the most widespread annoyances, irrespective of group size, is when members who have not finished the book complain about plot spoilers in the discussion, or get bored and want to talk about other things. A quarter of those who left a former book club due to dissatisfaction cited frustration over members not attending meetings or attending without having read the book as a factor in their decision.

The common refrain when it comes to many book club issues, including this one, is to firm up expectations. If expectations weren't clear before, make them clear now. **If the current expectations aren't working, set new ones.** Some groups have a rule that members must have finished the book to attend a meeting. Some are accepting of members attending without having read the book but specify that it is not acceptable to prevent others from discussing it in full. One member says, "Our rule is that you are always welcome to attend book club but if you haven't read the book you may only listen. We agreed that we would not curtail discussion to accommodate those who have not read or finished the book. We un-invited a member who did not read the books."

Talk about what particular problems your group is having around people not reading the books, and match expectations for future participation to your needs.

Improving Book Selection

Selecting good books to read and discuss is of critical importance to the success of a book club. Fourteen percent of those in a book club have experienced book selection issues, and disagreements over book selection was a factor for 26% of those who left a former book club due to dissatisfaction. Common frustrations include:

- Members who don't participate in suggesting books. This can lead to burnout in those who do participate, and may limit the variety of book selections. Some people (particularly those who are official or de facto leaders of their group) feel that the burden of book selection is falling too heavily on too few shoulders. Conversely, others are frustrated that just one or a few members select the books and would like to have a more inclusive process.

- The selection process being too time-consuming.

- Book choices being too limited in terms of genre, or not sufficiently challenging.

- Low-quality books being read, often because members suggest them without reading (or even researching) them first.

If the current book selection process isn't working for your group, consider making a change in how and when you select books. Below are approaches that have worked for other groups and may work for yours, too.

Take Turns

In 32% of private book clubs and 12% of public groups, members take turns picking a book. Some commented that choosing books this way has proven helpful in adding variety to their group's reading. One member says, "We previously tried to make suggestions and have the group agree but that led to some people dictating our reading schedule and the books being similar. So now we take it in turns to select books. This approach has worked well."

Put It to a Vote or Discussion

In 62% of private book clubs and 55% of public groups, all members can suggest book titles, and the group as a whole decides which to read. There are many variations on this process. Some groups ask members to introduce their book suggestion(s) and say a few words, or write a short description; others prefer suggestions to be anonymous. Respondents who favor the latter approach say that anonymous recommendations reduce the anxiety of suggesting a book only to have it rejected. However, this limits the opportunity for people to advocate for their particular recommendations, or for the group to be reassured that the person making the recommendation has actually read or researched the book. So each group has to feel out what works for them.

Some engage in discussion before voting, others don't. **Some vote openly, others have secret ballots.** One member says, "We are 7 members and we choose 3-4 books at a time. Anyone can make suggestions (but not all do) and then we discuss and decide which we want to read. We've found the discussion takes too long if we try to pick more than this many books at a time." Another approach: "We all suggest books and say a few words about them, then the members privately rate them on a 1-10 scale. This helps us select books that most members want to read and gives everyone a voice in the process."

Some groups have rules about who can suggest books. For example, some clubs don't allow new members or members who don't attend meetings regularly to be involved in the book selection process.

Organize a Schedule for Picking Books

Many groups have settled on a process whereby book selection takes place at designated times of the year. Often, members come to these meetings with one or more book suggestions, and then the titles are discussed and agreed upon.

Screen Selections

Some groups stipulate that the person proposing a book for discussion needs to have read it, or at least to have done sufficient research to justify the selection. One member comments, "To guarantee good selections, choosers of books must either be familiar with the author, read reviews from good sources or read at least a portion of the book before recommending it."

Expand Your Horizons

A significant number of people we surveyed say that their group's book selections are not sufficiently challenging. **Frequent comments include a desire for the group to read outside their comfort zone and from a wider range of genres, particularly nonfiction.**

Disappointments may sometimes come about due to the conflicting desires of those responsible for picking books. When asked to describe what they look for in a book for discussion, 57% of book clubbers say they would like it to be in a genre different from what their group has recently read, and 73% want their group to be challenged by it. But the overwhelming majority, 96%, also want it to be a book the group will enjoy. The desire to pick a book that will be liked can override the desire to explore new reading avenues. This may result in book recommendations too similar to ones the group has previously enjoyed — paradoxically, members of the group end up dissatisfied because they feel insufficiently challenged.

Book club members often state that many of their best discussions have been about books that elicited strongly divergent opinions precisely because not everyone liked them. One member says, "Sometimes the best discussions are about books where some people love it and some hate it. We have learned to laugh when some people dislike the book. It just makes for a better discussion."

Adjusting Group Size

We've talked about how group size is an important factor in a book club, but how do you get your club to the size you want? What if your club has grown to a size that's become unwieldy, or shrunk to such a degree that discussions just aren't very interesting?

Group Too Small

We found that 14% of book clubs have experienced problems with being too small and/or finding new members. Sometimes a group simply has too few participants for a good discussion; other times, the group itself may not be overly small but members would like to introduce new perspectives. Over time, book clubs can consolidate to a core group who tend to have similar reading tastes and opinions, and introducing new members can shake things up, adding diversity of opinions and reading interests, which may lead to more fulfilling discussions. Some feel that their club's discussions would be improved if they could broaden a specific demographic of their group, such as by attracting younger members, or more ethnic or gender diversity. Others simply wish to introduce new voices.

Expanding your numbers

Book clubs employ various strategies to boost membership. **The majority of clubs gain new members through word-of-mouth.** Some use social networking, or advertise locally. Strategies members recall working include:

- Having each existing member ask a friend or acquaintance to join.

- Promoting the club at the local library.

- Hosting an event to attract new members: "We hosted a summer potluck where members invited others to come and decide if they would like to join."

Expanding for diversity

For clubs seeking greater diversity, **consider what your group can offer new members who don't fit your current demographics.** This is especially important if the demographics the club is missing or seeking are marginalized ones. As addressed in the second of our "Questions to Answer When Starting a Book Club" in the Starting or Joining a Book Club chapter, people from minority or marginalized backgrounds may understandably steer clear of groups whose politics and values don't align with their own or aren't clearly stated, as these factors can affect how they expect to be seen and treated. For this reason, making space for diversity takes more (and, in fact, a markedly different approach) than simply saying that everyone is welcome. For more on making your book club an inclusive and welcoming space, see "How to Have a Sensitive and Respectful Discussion" in the Preparing for and Having Successful Discussions chapter.

In addition to considering diversity in factors like race, ethnicity, gender identity, and sexual orientation, **think about how accessible your club is to members who are disabled or face financial or time-related barriers.** Among people we surveyed who said that they were interested in being in a book club but weren't currently, 39% stated the primary reason for not being in a group as not having time or otherwise not being able to.

> *"Transportation and child care are sometimes difficult to plan."* — Female, aged 35-44, reads 2 books/month

> *"I have a visual handicap, plus transportation is a problem."* — Female, aged 65-74, reads 5-6 books/month

> *"I'd be interested but I'd be worried they'd all read too quickly, I'm a slow reader because of my dyslexia."* — Female, aged 55-64, reads about 2 books/month

How could your book club accommodate the readers above? How can potential members with similar or related concerns know that you will accommodate them? Thinking about these questions and coming up with answers can be a step in the right direction to making your club more accessible. Another step that may help some clubs become more accessible to a greater variety of members is to go virtual (or hybrid) with meetings, which we'll discuss in the next chapter.

Integrating new members

Once you find new members, you'll need to successfully introduce them into the group. Four percent of those currently in private book clubs and 5% of those in public groups say their group has had issues integrating new members. Integration can be a challenge for a new person, who may feel like an outsider. It can also be a challenge for existing members if the dynamics of the group shift significantly. Some of those who left a book club due to dissatisfaction did so because they felt the group dynamics had changed for the worse with the introduction of new members. This is one of the reasons why book clubs need to talk about and agree on how they want their group to run — so that expectations are clear for both new and existing members. **Try to strike a balance between emphasizing expectations and giving new people time to adjust.**

To that end, here are some approaches members describe their clubs having taken:

> *"New people are given leeway as they get used to the group norms. We provide in-person and email guidance to help them feel comfortable."*

> *"We invite a new guest for two meetings in a row. Then the group votes at the next meeting to determine if the guest becomes a member."*

Group Too Big

Ten percent of private book club members, and 4% of those in public groups, say that their book club has encountered problems due to the group getting too big. The optimal size for a book club depends on many factors, but issues tend to emerge when clubs exceed the optimal size for their format, such as:

- Difficulties finding venues/the group being too big for some members to host at home.

- Declining participation in discussions because the more vocal members tend to overwhelm quieter ones.

- An increase in side conversations.

- Meetings running too long.

Members suggest a variety of solutions, which fall into three broad categories:

- Have an agreed-upon cap for membership and, if necessary, a waiting list.

- Split the group into two.

- Maintain a single book club but with concurrent independent discussions.

Cooling Down Competitive Hosting

For many, food is an integral part of the book club experience. After all, food is closely tied with social gatherings, and book clubs are no exception. In fact, 91% of private book clubs have food at their meetings, ranging from a snack (41%) to a full host-cooked meal (13%) or potluck (13%). Among public book clubs, 61% have some sort of food but the vast majority keep it very simple. While many people we surveyed commented that book clubs are a place to connect with their community while sharing good food, the responsibilities involved can become a point of contention among members, particularly when the inclusion of food spurs competitive hosting. When members take turns hosting or bringing food to a meeting, it's easy for each person to feel that they need to match or improve upon the previous offerings, and before you know it, bringing the "snack" has gone from being fun to being a cause of stress.

So what can you do if you feel your book club suffers from competitive hosting? You could take the lead and the next time it's your turn to host, provide something simple but tasty, like cheese and crackers or a plate of vegetables and a dip, taking the pressure off the next person. But if the group has become accustomed to elaborate eats this might not go down well. We recommend you follow the example of groups who have successfully resolved this issue by **having an open discussion on the topic and, if most of the group feels the same way, simply agreeing to cut back on the hosting!**

One member stated, "We found that some of us were guilty of overdoing the 'snacks' and producing full meals, so we dialed back on cooking efforts, so as not to create a competitive atmosphere for hosts."

Another option some clubs have found success with is **simply limiting the amount of hosting a single member has to do, keeping hosting duties for each person to once or twice a year.**

Some groups organize themed potlucks or other meetings where food is a major focus, but only occasionally. If your group members like to flex their culinary muscles, you could suggest that the food for the meetings generally be kept simple, but that every now and then you have a themed get-together based on the particular book you're discussing — for example, with everyone providing a dish appropriate to the period or geographical setting of the book. Members can even bring guests and have an all-out party. Then next month you can get back to the cheese and crackers!

Confronting Problematic Members Sensitively and Asking Members to Leave

Six percent of those currently in private book clubs and 4% of those in public groups say their book club has had to ask one or more members to leave. In their open-ended responses, some other respondents noted that one or more people voluntarily left their book club after the group failed to resolve a disagreement.

Generally, asking a member to leave a group is not a step taken lightly, and often only considered when things have reached the point where other members of the group are starting to drift away. Sometimes the issue is relatively clear-cut because it relates to the book club's rules; for example, a member who either regularly misses meetings or doesn't read the book in a group that expects one or both from its members. Other times, it might be because a member is consistently disruptive.

One book clubber says, "We've talked about people talking among themselves while we are having a discussion; always the same few people. I am the facilitator and have asked a few people to leave the club because of this."

Sometimes, given the choice between changing their habits or leaving, a member will choose to leave the group. Or it simply becomes clear to the member that they are not a good fit and they decide to move on of their own accord. Book club members' comments show that respectfully confronting problematic members is possible, and that once they have been confronted, the situation may effectively take care of itself:

> *"One member was disrespectful to the other members and to our guest authors. I sent them an email letting them know their behavior could not continue. If they were disrespectful just one more time, I would ask them to leave the group. The person never acknowledged my email, nor came back."*
>
> *"One previous member thought she was more intelligent than us and would let us know how she felt! We confronted her and eventually she quit the group."*
>
> *"Once in a while a new member wants to transform the group. The moderator talks with them personally (often over lunch or coffee) encouraging them to find a group that better fits their needs."*

Some groups who fail to resolve a problem with a member either end up continuing with the challenging member(s) or disbanding. Sometimes a group that disbands will reform later without the difficult member(s).

What seems clear in all this is that the long-term happiness of the club is almost always affected by problematic members, so it's better to address a situation than hope it goes away. **When confronting a member about their behavior or asking them to leave, consider contacting them through email or by having one person speak to them privately outside of meetings.** This gives the person space to absorb the information rather than feeling they need to react to it, and they're more likely to either adjust to expectations or quietly leave the club.

Why People Leave Book Clubs

Ultimately if book club issues go on for long enough without being addressed, your members may decide to leave. Understanding why members generally decide to leave book clubs can help you keep your own club together.

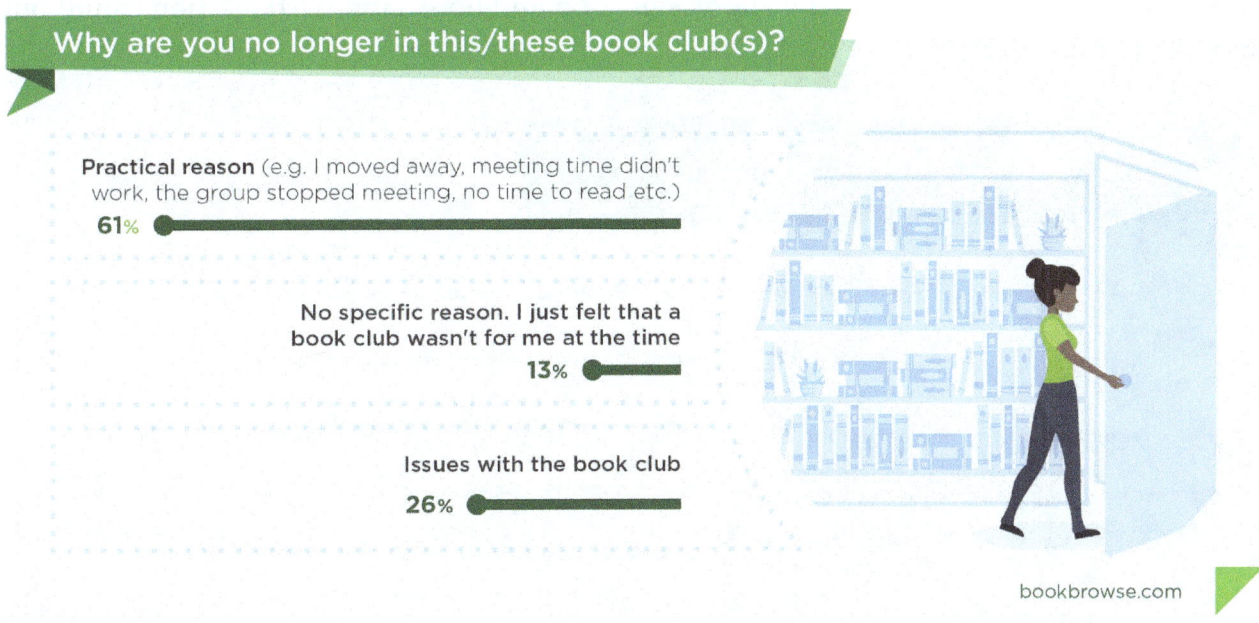

In our research, only 26% of respondents left their book clubs because of a specific issue or issues, and this wasn't an easy decision: 65% of participants had been in their clubs for over a year when they decided to leave.

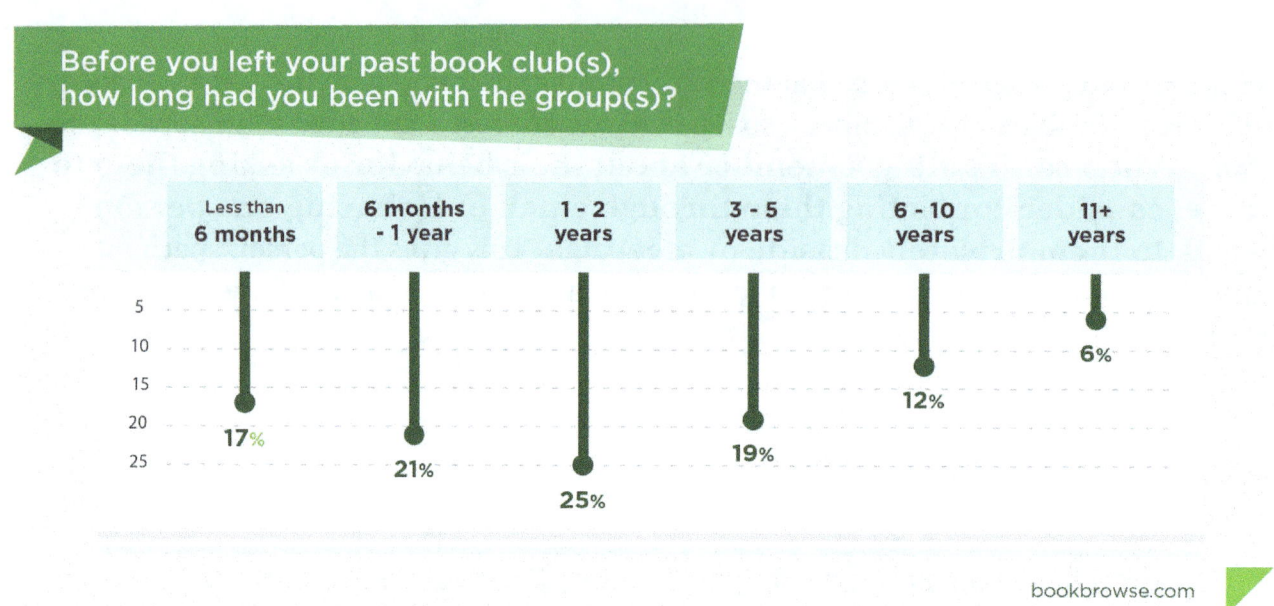

By far the most common reason for leaving a book club due to dissatisfaction was an overly dominant personality, while book selection and book club participation round out the top 3.

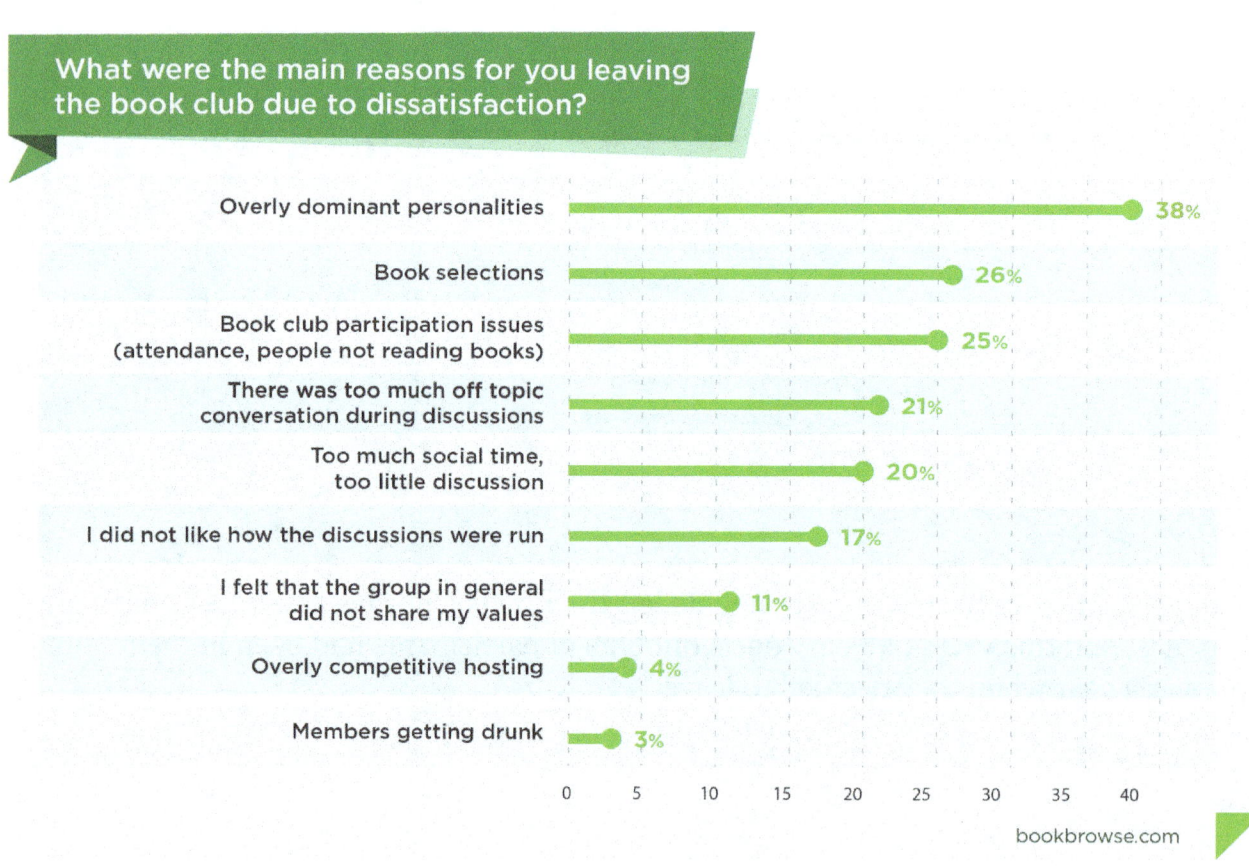

From this data we have two recommendations:

- **Perform a Book Club Health Check at least annually.** As 65% of members leave after one year, the Health Check provides an opportunity to identify issues prior to members leaving.

- **Conduct Exit Surveys.** If a member does decide to leave, conducting a short survey or exit interview with them can help you identify why they're leaving, but it can also be an opportunity to get honest feedback about the club, as the former member no longer has to worry about ruffled feathers. While we encourage you to have an in person conversation, potentially over coffee or a meal, a template email is included at the end of the book.

Chapter 6: Virtual Book Clubs

Why Go Virtual with Your Book Club?

Virtual book clubs, or book groups that meet virtually rather than in person, are a great option for expanding membership across distances and keeping discussions open to a wider variety of participants. Reasons why members might need or prefer a virtual club include a lack of transportation, being pressed for time, simple convenience, disabilities that make both public and private places less accessible, social anxiety, and the risk of airborne illness. Virtual groups became more popular during the lockdown phase of the Covid-19 pandemic, and online connections and communities continue to be vital lifelines for many current and potential members of book clubs. Even if your club prefers to meet in person, considering the possibility of hybrid meetings, with members having the option to attend virtually, can help accommodate the needs of new members along with existing ones.

Tools for Online Book Clubs

Private Groups for Posting and Commenting

To hold your club discussions online in a simple posting and commenting forum, you can easily create a private group on Facebook[32] or Goodreads[33], which is especially convenient if most of your club members are already on one of these sites.

One advantage to moving your club to these platforms is that you don't have to set specific meeting times. However, you'll probably still find some degree of planning helpful to maintaining enthusiasm and smooth communication. To stay organized, **set a clear time limit** on each book discussion. In general, it's probably a good idea for discussions to last at least a week, as conversations move slower when multiple people are responding to each other at different times.

You may also want to lay down some ground rules for posting. For example, you can **designate one person to get the discussion off to a strong start** by creating multiple posts, each with a different question or discussion prompt. Then everyone is free to comment on whatever posts they want, first taking in what others have said, just as you would in an in-person discussion. Alternately or additionally, you can make it a different person's job to introduce new topics every day for as long as the discussion lasts. Really, this all just depends on what your group is comfortable with, and especially with smaller groups, it may be best to simply improvise and see what works.

Note: In addition to the regular posting and commenting features on Facebook, you can use Facebook Messenger[34] for group chats, group audio calls, and group video chats (more on this coming up next).

Group Text Chats

Apps that give you the ability to group chat through typed or texted instant messages, like WhatsApp[35] and Facebook Messenger[36], are great for clubs that would like to hold discussions in real time while avoiding the technology blips that video conferencing might involve.

The biggest challenge with group chats is that they can move very quickly, making it difficult to keep up or get a word in edgewise. To prevent this, limit the group size for each chat. If you have a club of more than five or six members, it may be wise to split up into two or more separate discussion groups.

To keep discussions from getting too cluttered, introduce topics one at a time. Try loosely planning out the conversation ahead of time and emailing a list of questions or topics to everyone, or let members collaborate by writing out their own ideas for discussion in a Google Doc. Once a topic is introduced, people can chat freely until the conversation begins to die down, then move on to the next topic.

Video and Audio Calls

Another increasingly popular option for meetings and communication in general is group video or audio conferencing through services like Facebook Messenger[37], Zoom[38], Microsoft Teams[39], and Google Meet[40]. FaceTime[41] is also a good platform for group meetings but requires someone with an Apple device to initiate the call, which may be a dealbreaker for some book groups.

Using **video group chats** for your book discussions can create a more "normal" discussion atmosphere but might also require time to get comfortable. You may want to **set up a practice meeting ahead of time** where instead of having a focused discussion, you just check in to see how everyone is doing and get familiar with the platform's features. Once you start your regular club meetings, you can **choose a leader for each meeting** to plan and guide discussions so that people don't have to think too much about when to speak or what to talk about.

Group audio calls may be the most challenging book discussion format to pull off, since it can be difficult to coordinate a conversation with a whole group of people and no visual cues. The main benefit of audio calls over video is that they're often less prone to glitches and other technical issues. Group audio will likely work best for small clubs where everyone is already comfortable with each other. Even then, you may want to make it one person's role to ask questions that make it easy for people to indicate they have something to say before sharing their thoughts. For example, the person might introduce a topic and then ask, "Does anyone have thoughts on that?"

Suggestions for Hybrid Discussion

If you do decide to do a hybrid book club discussion, having the remote participants use a video call software is usually better than relying on audio only, for the same reasons given above. When using a video call tool, it's best if the 'in person' camera is set up so that as many of the in-person participants can be seen, for example at the end of a long table.

It's also best to give the remote participants instructions for 'raising their hand', and many tools today have built in features for participants to flag when they'd like to speak. Otherwise it can be hard for the remote participants to compete with in-person participants who are able to visually cue when they want to speak. The facilitator should pay special attention that the remote participants are speaking as much as they would like in the discussion, and the facilitator should also confirm that the remote participants can hear the in person discussion (some of the quieter participants may need to speak up or sit closer to the mic). If the remote participants get disconnected or frozen, it's ok to pause the discussion for a moment or two to troubleshoot, but if the problems persist it's best to keep the discussion moving and then summarize the discussion once the remote participants are able to reconnect.

When considering any of the above advice, keep in mind that while rules and guidelines can be helpful, they should facilitate communication rather than making it more restricted. Don't be afraid to experiment, be flexible, and have fun!

Public Virtual Book Clubs

If you aren't currently in a book club, or are just interested in expanding your virtual book group options, you can always explore existing public clubs online.

First, it's possible that **your local library** already runs one or multiple public book groups online, so it may be worth checking to see what's available.

Some bookstores host discussions virtually. For example, Bel Canto Books[42] in Long Beach, California, founded by poet Jhoanna Belfer, has multiple book clubs, some of which offer virtual meetings. Many events like this cost nothing and simply require you to register ahead of time. Just be sure to read and follow any rules the virtual book club has for participating in discussions, and support stores by buying from them whenever you can!

Goodreads maintains a database of virtual book groups[43], many of them public and open for anyone to join. On BookClubs.com[44] you can search for in-person and online clubs that are open to the public and looking for new members by topic, book, or location.

At BookBrowse, we hold regular book club discussions in our community forum, where members can create their own posts or topic threads and reply to others. Books are given for free to BookBrowse members who opt to read them in exchange for trying their best to participate in the discussion. Check out our current and past online discussions[45] to see which titles we've chosen to feature.

Bonus Option: Postal Book Clubs

Here's another interesting option for long-distance book discussions with which you may be less familiar. In a **postal book club**, books and journals are cycled through a group of people via mail, giving everyone a chance to read and record their thoughts on each book before sending it on to the next recipient. This system bypasses many of the logistical problems book clubs typically deal with: sourcing copies of a book for multiple people, setting meeting times that work for everyone, making sure all members have enough of a chance to participate. But it does come with its own challenges, and requires commitment to the format. Postal book clubs can be organized through Goodreads or other online platforms. To start your own, create a public post that mentions how many members you're looking for, what kind of mailing schedule you anticipate, and other specifics.

In an interview with BookBrowse[46], Linda, a longtime postal book club participant, explains how the process works for her group: "There are six people in our postal book group. My group is all from the U.S., but I know of others who have people from other countries included. In our group, each person picks a book of no more than 300 pages, roughly—320 pages is okay, 400 not so much—and makes notes in a journal about why they picked that particular book and then adds comments and opinions of the book. The book and the journal are mailed to the next person on the list. That next person reads the book and notes their comments and opinions in the journal and sends it to the third person. The book stays with each person for two months, so by the end of a year each of us have read six books and each person has their book back. Then we start a new round and the original journal goes around again. This gives everyone in the group the opportunity to see what others wrote about the previous book."

She also offers a useful piece of advice: "*The* important thing is to keep communication open. I let the next person know if the book will be a little late. The person who sends to me does the same."

Chapter 7: Extra, Extra! Ideas to Enhance Your Book Club

Book Club Food Ideas

We've already discussed the dangers of overdoing it with the book club consumables, but that's no reason to cut out food entirely, right? Regardless of what level of hosting, dining, or ordering out your club enjoys, we have some fresh food ideas for you. In our research, we asked book club members what snacks or meals their groups prefer for their meetings. Here we share some of the most popular responses, along with suggestions and resources that you can use for cooking up fun, food-filled sessions with your club.

Of course, many clubs are online (and as we've pointed out, there are multiple reasons for book clubs to consider going virtual or hybrid). But meeting virtually doesn't mean you have to miss out on refreshments. Ordering, picking up, or preparing food separately can even create a connection to bridge the distance between members.

So here are some ideas for easy food inspiration. Bon appetit!

Make Something Easy and Shareable

Food ideas from book club members include shareable snacks such as cheese and crackers, charcuterie trays, and fruit and veggie arrangements.

Meals that are easy to separate into individual portions are also great for sharing. An especially beloved dish among book clubs is quiche. Pizza and pasta dishes are also popular standbys; as are hearty soups with bread, chili, baked potatoes with various toppings, and salads (perhaps a light green salad if contributing to a potluck, or something more robust like a bean or pasta salad if providing the main dish).

And book clubbers are particularly fond of dessert options of every type, including pies, cakes, muffins, lemon bars, and brownies.

For help preparing your own easy and shareable snacks, meals, and desserts, here are a few hearty recipe lists to peruse:

- "Tasty One-Bite Appetizer Recipes[47]" from *Taste of Home*

- "Dishes to Wow Your Book Club[48]" from Oprah.com
- "Easy desserts for effortless entertaining[49]" from *delicious*

Create Meals or Snacks (or Drinks) Based on the Book

Many groups plan meals based on the setting of the book they're discussing, or in some way match books with food. As fun as a themed spread can be, figuring out how exactly to bring it all together can be challenging, so here are a couple of resources to help.

Taste of Home provides a list of recipes[50] to pair with books your club may already be planning a meeting around, including Korean cream cheese garlic bread for Michelle Zauner's Crying in H Mart[51], a classic aviation cocktail for Sarah Penner's The Lost Apothecary[52], and nutty stuffed mushrooms for Cheryl Strayed's Wild[53].

The Book Club CookBook[54] makes it easy to browse book-related recipes by type (appetizers, entrees, etc.) or book title. You can also look through their impressive list of authors who have contributed to the site. Try your hand at Elizabeth Strout's recipe for her famous character Olive Kitteridge[55]'s grandmother's doughnuts; So You Want to Talk About Race[56] author Ijeoma Oluo's butterscotch "feminist pudding" (with optional bourbon); Alka Joshi's "royal" rabri (a North Indian dessert) as depicted in The Henna Artist[57]; or Amor Towles' Latvian stew, which he discovered in *Saveur* magazine and which later provided inspiration for a scene in A Gentleman in Moscow[58].

Support Your Local Restaurants

Taking the pressure off is one of the reasons some book clubs say that their group prefers to go the restaurant route all or some of the time. Another reason is that they like to match the restaurant to the setting of the book they're reading. But keep in mind that a noisy restaurant can make it difficult to hear each other, which is why some groups meet in the same restaurant or cafe each time, reserving a table that they know to be relatively quiet. Another option, of course, is ordering out or getting take-out. Overall, getting food from restaurants is convenient, and also a great way to accommodate dietary restrictions or preferences, as your group can take part in a low-effort shared experience while giving everyone the chance to choose their own meal.

Inviting Authors to Your Book Club

Inviting your favorite authors to chat with your book club doesn't have to remain a fantasy. Sure, asking an author to join your group for a discussion can seem intimidating. You might wonder how to even go about it. But it may be easier than you think! Let's consider the details.

You can often start by contacting an author through their website or social media. Some authors will state on their website that they are happy to chat with book clubs. The official website of historical fiction author Marie Benedict[59], a dream discussion guest for many groups, currently states that Marie is available to meet with book clubs in person or through Zoom. Some authors even provide a dedicated contact form for book clubs. But if an author's availability isn't clear, it's still worth sending them a note asking if they might be able to meet with your group. Many authors are active on one or more social media platforms, so you may be able to contact them by direct message.

In your first communication, tell the author which book you hope to discuss with them, and include some brief information about your group — such as how many members you have and where you're located.

Be respectful of their time and preferences. If an author has posted that they're open to meeting with book clubs, it's because they genuinely want to do so, but they undoubtedly have many demands on their time, so get in contact well ahead and be flexible. For example, if you invite the author to chat virtually and they can't make your regular meeting day and time, perhaps the group could meet specifically to talk with the author on a different day that works for everyone (or even most of you). Even if the author is local to you, they might prefer to meet virtually, and if they're not local, then some kind of video platform will likely be the best option (see the Virtual Book Clubs chapter).

If you organize a public book club, such as in a library or bookstore, and want to publicize the event, planning ahead can be especially crucial. For example, Terye Balogh of the Milpitas Library in California sometimes books authors a full year in advance, and always for the night when the book group regularly meets, so she can count on members to be available on that date to form the core of the audience. Terye shared her extensive experience with inviting authors and running a book club in an interview with BookBrowse[60].

Agree on the details, taking your lead from the author. Make sure that both parties are clear on the day and time (if chatting virtually, check your time zones), which book you want to talk about, and how long the author is available for. If meeting virtually, agree on the platform (e.g,. Zoom) and make sure to send the link at least a few days ahead, with a reminder on the day.

Discuss the book before meeting with the author. For example, ask the author to join you for the second half of your meeting and use the first half to discuss the book, or discuss it at one meeting and then invite the author to the next.

Whether you discuss the book and meet with the author at the same meeting or a different time, **invite the author to join your group at least 10 minutes after the meeting has started**, so that latecomers have time to arrive at an in-person meeting, or get logged in if meeting online and sort out any technical issues before the author arrives.

Think of some questions you'd like to ask the author, but first have a look around the web for easily available information. For example, if the author has a Q&A on their website, have all members of the group read it ahead of time so that you're not asking the same questions that have already been answered.

Thank the author for their time, and show your appreciation by supporting their book however you can. One of the best ways to give back to an author who visits with your club is to buy their book, if possible, and spread the word about it. For example, tell your book-loving friends, post a review and/or recommendation on social media, etc.

Mixing Things Up: Add-Ons and Alternatives for Book Club Meetings

During the lockdown phase of the COVID-19 pandemic, we advised book groups dealing with library closures on **how to get creative with their reading material and meetings.** Some of this advice continues to be relevant for clubs facing financial limitations and other access issues, or for groups who just want to mix things up!

Our suggestions, updated below, are all great alternatives for clubs unable to meet the time, planning, material, and physical requirements of a traditional book club — and fantastic for *any* club looking for ideas to keep their group fresh. These ideas could work especially well for virtual clubs.

Attend a Virtual Author Reading

Some book clubs enjoy attending author events as a supplement to reading a book. Author readings can also be an end in themselves, and a way to experience a piece of writing for the first time. With many events now offering a virtual option, finding and attending them is much easier. Bookstores and libraries across the country (and the world) live-stream (and record) authors reading their writing — for example, excerpts from a novel, a short story, or poems. Often, you can reserve a "ticket" at no cost (or for a suggested donation if you can afford it) and connect through a video platform when the event begins.

Have all your book club members reserve places for a reading in advance.
You could either pair this activity with reading an author's book, or make it a replacement for reading the book, and discuss the event afterwards. This can be a big timesaver, as you don't need to budget the time to read a whole book, and may be useful for book clubs with busy members who struggle with the commitment of choosing and sourcing books.

Alternatively, many past author events are available on YouTube[61] and can be viewed at any time.

Publisher, author, and bookstore websites are great places to find upcoming and past readings.

Pick a Topic or Genre

Instead of the group picking a single title to read, agree on a topic, theme, or genre (as broad as necessary), and you can each **choose a relevant title from your own bookshelves**. For example, a memoir, a novel that qualifies as a mystery or thriller, a book set in a particular time or place.

You could start your meeting with everyone taking turns introducing their book and explaining why they chose it, and then open up the conversation to discuss similarities between the books. For example, if comparing amateur detective novels, you could discuss whether there are characteristics that the detectives generally have in common, or what draws you as a reader to the genre. You could also compare and contrast the writing styles — e.g., discussing books narrated in the third person compared to first-person voice, or whether books are character- or action-driven.

Share What You're Reading Now

Many successful book clubs never read the same book, but simply get together regularly to discuss and recommend books they've recently read. So instead of picking one book for everyone to read that you all have to track down a copy of, you can simply come to the meeting ready to tell the group about a book of your choice. (You might want to coordinate ahead of time to make sure multiple people don't pick the same book to talk about.)

All the World's a Stage

The line between literature and drama has always been a fine one. Rather than reading a book, watch a play and discuss it together! Playbill[62] offers a schedule of upcoming and current free live-streamed broadcasts from theaters all over the world.

Take Inspiration From the Literary Salons of Old

The salons of yesteryear didn't limit themselves to discussing books. Instead, they discussed ideas in general. If you want to meet regularly with your club but are limited by time, money, or other constraints, consider changing things up every few meetings or so. For example, you could pick a philosophical topic or two, encourage members to do background reading, and then meet to share your thoughts. You might already have discussed a particular topic in your book club at some point, but by removing the book from the equation, you'll be free to explore it as broadly as you want.

Even More "Extra": Fun Things to Do with Your Book Club

While many groups stick to the basics of reading and discussing books, some who have the time and inclination take things a little further, whether that means extending their love for books to food, games, and travel, or simply taking pleasure in being together in different settings. In our research, we asked people about what additional activities their clubs like to do. Answers covered a variety of pastimes both inside and outside of regular book club meetings, book-related and otherwise. If you're looking for ideas or inspiration to enhance your group's time together, or you're just curious about what other book clubs do, check out our summary of the results.

Getting Out and Going Places

Many book club members say that their book groups enjoy outings, often with a cultural or food-related focus. Art galleries and museums proved to be popular destinations, as did movies, plays, restaurants, and winery tours. Some clubs make these outings reading- or author-centered — attending writer talks, book festivals, or other literary events — while others like to engage in different activities entirely. In some cases, groups go so far as to plan full vacations or weekend trips, either to visit book-related sites or just to get away together.

Specific events and places that members mentioned include the Oregon Shakespeare Festival, a Van Gogh exhibit, afternoon tea at a hotel, the *L.A. Times* Festival of Books, and the homes of literary figures such as Edith Wharton, Mark Twain, and Robert Frost. Some groups have traveled to settings that appear in books. One member's club went to New York's Morgan Library & Museum in connection with The Personal Librarian[63]; others had visited sites related to Frank Lloyd Wright after reading Loving Frank[64].

Celebrating

Book groups also meet up to celebrate holidays, anniversaries, or other events. Annual get-togethers are popular among book clubs, as is celebrating members' birthdays, and commemorating milestones like reading a certain number of books or being together for a certain number of years. Many clubs host gift or book exchanges at holiday or end-of-year events.

Volunteer and Community Work

A substantial number of members say that their group supports their local community or causes they care about; activities include donating books to a library, cooking at a women's shelter, supporting people in need, and hosting speakers at book-related events. Additionally, many groups make a point of frequenting local businesses, such as restaurants and independent bookstores.

Enjoying Time Together in Other Ways

Getting together for a meal, a movie, or just to socialize is an option that many enjoy. As with some ideas we've already discussed in this chapter and previous ones, groups may still connect these get-togethers to books in some way — watching a film adaptation of a book, playing games related to books, meeting for book-themed food, or inviting an author to a meeting — but some opt to reserve time for unrelated activities or conversation, whether surrounding film, TV, current events, or other subjects. Additional group activities that book club members enjoy together, whether book-focused or not, include coloring, cooking, knitting, painting, and crafts.

Turning the Page: The Possibilities of Book Clubs

We hope this book has been useful to you in negotiating the basics of starting and maintaining a book club. We also hope you've found it as inspiring as we have to consider all the possibilities of what a book club can look like and achieve. In an age when the practical utility of reading is often questioned, it's heartening to see that when put into the dynamic setting of a discussion group, books are not only likely to expand our viewpoints and change us as people, but to give us the grounding and resources necessary to take action, together and separately, in our own lives and on a larger scale, in all kinds of ways.

Book Clubs on the Rise

While there is a prevailing narrative that reading culture may be in decline in the US, BookBrowse's own research and publicly available data suggest otherwise.

In 2022, The Census Bureau administered the Survey of Public Participation in the Arts[65], which, among other findings, discovered that "At roughly 5 percent...the share of adults who participated in book clubs or reading groups did not change significantly from five years earlier."

Meanwhile, the 2020 Census [66]found the adult population to be 258 million. So, factoring in some population growth, a 5% estimate of the adult population gets us to 13 million book clubbers!

Based on BookBrowse's research, book club participation is continuing to increase.

In our 2025 book club survey of roughly 1000 respondents, we asked book clubbers whether or not they thought book club participation was increasing (their perception), as well as what was actually happening within their own groups:

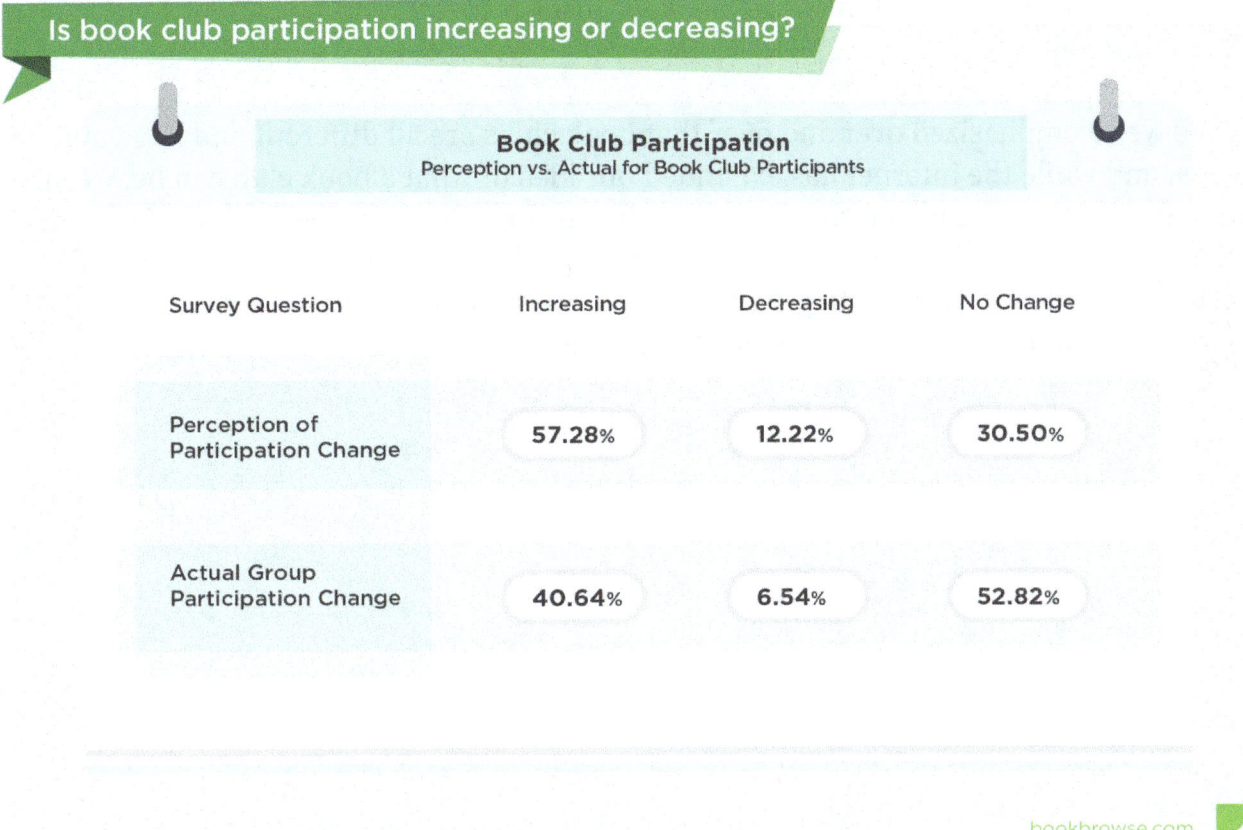

So, good news! While our data is a smaller sample, it shows book club participation increasing, which aligns with other reporting.

Final Thoughts

Now more than ever, book groups can be flexible, accessible, and specific to their members' lives and needs. While certain stereotypes and narrow ideas of book clubs may persist, these have always been countered by real-life groups that don't fit those perceptions, and new and exciting developments in how we relate to each other continue to pave the way forward. With the option to start and maintain clubs in a virtual or a hybrid setting, the future of book clubs is wide open.

Regardless of what groups are taking new members in your community, and no matter where you live, you can create your ideal club as you see fit. Make sure to bring the wine — or don't. Serve cheese and crackers, or cook up an elaborate feast. Meet on a weeknight to discuss local politics alongside a recent nonfiction book, or over brunch on the weekend to chat about the latest big romance or historical novel. Gather online with others from all over the country and world, or meet in a park with your neighbors.

Require that everyone read the same book, or just get together to talk about what you're all reading now.

While we've emphasized over and over that book clubs are all different and have unique needs, and while the internet has expanded our idea of what a book club can be, we also think it's worth pointing out that there's really nothing else like a book club. No other group or gathering of people quite offers the same blend of intimacy, openness, and purpose, and the particular purpose of your group is up to you. No matter what it is, we're honored to be part of your book club journey.

Book Club Resources

To assist you with your book groups, we've assembled template resources in the back of this book:

- **Key Questions to Answer When Starting a Book Club**

- **The Book Club Health Check Template**

- **Book Club Discussion Prep Worksheet**

- **Book Club Facilitator Worksheet**

- **Example Exit Survey Email**

Accessing Support Group & Book Club Resources Electronically

Included with your purchase is access to the *A Club of One's Own* support group, where you can ask questions and share resources with fellow book club leaders, and you can also access copies of our resources electronically to download or customize them. Follow the instructions below:

1. If you don't already have a BookBrowse membership, join at bookbrowse.com/join[67]. Note that you do not need to pay for an account, we offer free accounts at: bookbrowse.com/join/free_signup.cfm[68]. You will need an account in order to access the forum.

2. If you purchased *A Club of One's Own* via BookBrowse.com you should've already received an invitation to join the private section of the BookBrowse forum dedicated to *A Club of One's Own*, if you purchased *A Club of One's Own* elsewhere or did not receive an invite, please email proof of purchase to cs@bookbrowse.com[69] and we'll send an invite to that section of the forum.

3. Once you accept the invite you should be able to access the private section of the forum, either by searching for 'A Club of One's Own' in the search bar at community.bookbrowse.com, or by going to bookbrowse.com/bcref[70], you will find links to google doc copies of each resource.

The Key Questions to Answer When Starting a Book Club

1. When will you meet and for how long?

_____

_____

2. Who do you want in the group?

_____

_____

3. How many people?

_____

_____

4. How important is book discussion to your group?

_____

_____

5. What do you want to read and how will you choose books?

_____

_____

6. Do you want someone to lead the discussion?

_____

_____

_____

7. How many books do you want to read and how often do you want to meet?

_____

_____

_____

8. Where will you meet?

_____

_____

_____

9. Does your group want to wait to read in paperback/cheaper ebook format?

_____

_____

_____

10. Will there be food at your meetings?

_____

_____

_____

11. How will you contact members?

_____

_____

_____

The Book Club Health Check Template

Instructions: Please take a moment to reflect on your experience with your book club. For each statement, rate your level of agreement on a scale of **1 to 5**, where:

- 1 = **Strongly Disagree**
- 2 = **Disagree**
- 3 = **Neutral**
- 4 = **Agree**
- 5 = **Strongly Agree**

Once you're finished, total your score and flip over to continue the health check. For best results, **do not check the back before completing the first part of this assessment.**

	Statement	Rating (1–5)
1	The meeting **frequency, time, and location(s)** work well for me.	_____
2	I am satisfied with member **attendance and book completion**.	_____
3	I'm satisfied with the **types of books** we read and the **selection process**.	_____
4	The club is a **good size**, and I'm happy with the **mix of members**.	_____
5	There is a **good balance** between **book discussion** and **social time**.	_____
6	I find our **discussions engaging and satisfying**.	_____
7	The group is **well-organized** with **effective scheduling and communication**.	_____
8	There are **no overly dominant personalities** that negatively impact the group.	_____
9	Members have enough **opportunity to contribute** to the discussion.	_____
10	I feel **comfortable and welcome** in our book club.	_____

11   The book club is **meeting my expectations and goals** as a   _____
     participant.

12   I would not change anything about the group.   _____

                          Add Your Ratings for Your Total Score: _____

Assessment Results Based on Total Score:

48 and Above: Your book club is in great shape. There may be a few opportunities to work on, but overall things are going well.

42 to 47: Your book club is going pretty well, but there are likely some concerns that should be addressed.

Less than 41: There are issues with your book club that should be addressed. Consider raising your concerns if you feel comfortable.

Based on the score on your first page, do you agree with the above assessment of your club? (circle one).

Yes   No

Would you like to provide additional context for how you feel about how things are going with your book club?

_____

_____

_____

For answers on the first page that you rated 3 or lower, what could be done to improve your rating?

_____

_____

_____

Book Club Discussion Prep Worksheet

Book Title: _____

Date and Time of Book Club Meeting: _____

Why did you / your book club choose this book?

_____

_____

_____

What were your expectations prior to reading?

_____

_____

_____

What are your first impressions after the first few pages?

_____

_____

_____

Key Characters and Relationships

You can list characters and take notes here, as well as note arcs and include relevant quotes.

_____

_____

_____

Major Themes & Symbols

Beyond the plot, what is the book about? What are recurring themes or issues that arise, and what quotes really hit these home?

_____
_____
_____

Discussion Questions

What do you want the groups' opinion on? Was there anything you personally were conflicted or unsure about? You can add questions using our question bank as well.

_____
_____
_____

Beyond the Book

Are there any historical or cultural contexts you want to discuss? What about related topics, or articles, author interviews, etc.?

_____
_____
_____

Personal Takeaways

What did you think about the book? What did you learn or feel? How does it compare to other books you've read? Would you recommend it to a friend? Why or why not?

_____

_____

_____

Book Club Facilitator Worksheet

Book Title: _____

Specific goal for the discussion?

_____

_____

_____

How much time are you allocating for book discussion? _____

Icebreaker Question or Opening Remarks?

_____

_____

_____

Known issues to be mindful of during discussion?

_____

_____

_____

Member Participation Tracking:

Member Name	Number of Comments

Tracking Discussion Length by Question:

Question Number	Minutes Spent on Question / Notes

Question Bank

Add your own questions ahead of time

General Book Club Questions

- What did you like best/least about the book, and why?
- Did you have expectations of the book (e.g., from reading reviews, hearing from friends)? If so, did it fall short, meet expectations, or exceed them?
- What do you think of the book title and jacket cover? Do you think they adequately reflect the book's content, or are they misleading? If you had creative control, what changes would you make, if any?
- Are you glad you read the book?
- What did you learn from the book? Did it change your perception? Did it leave you with questions you want to find answers to?
- Do you have a favorite quote or scene from the book? Why does this stand out to you?
- How do you think the book will age (or has aged)? If the book is recently published: Do you think it is one that people will still be reading in decades to come? If it was published in the past: Is it still relevant? If it was written now, how would it be different?
- Have you read other books on the same topic? If so, which would you recommend?
- What did you think of the book's ending?
- What audience would you recommend the book to?

- If you were making a movie of the book, who would you cast?

Book Club Questions About the Author or Their Writing

- Why do you think the author chose to write this particular book? What are they trying to convey, and are they successful in doing so?
- How would you describe the author's writing style? What did you like or not like about it?
- Does the author's writing style remind you of any other authors? If so, in what ways?
- If you were writing this book, would you tell the story the same way?
- If you could ask the author one question, what would it be?

Book Club Questions Focused on the Book's Story

- Was the story credible? For example, even in a fantasy setting, the characters' motives and actions need to make sense within the context of their world.
- What did you think of the pacing of the book? Did it hold your interest throughout? Were some parts too fast or slow?
- Did the author use symbolism? If so, what was the purpose of the symbolism? What was the author trying to convey?
- Did the plot proceed as you expected? What parts of it surprised you, if any?
- Did you wholly trust the narrator(s), or did you consider them unreliable in any way?

Book Club Questions About the Book's Characters

- Did you relate to a particular character or the circumstances they were in?
- Which character would you most like to meet? Why?
- How does the person (or people) who relate(s) the story color the telling?
- If the story had been told from a different perspective, what would have been different? Would you have liked to hear from another character?
- Are the characters believable? For example, does a child narrator sound the age they are? Does the voice of a character in a historical novel seem true to the period? Do you think it's meant to?
- If you were the main character, would you have acted as they did?
- What do you imagine might happen to the characters after the story ends?

Book Club Questions for the Book's Setting

- How well did the author paint a picture of the setting?
- How did the setting impact the story? If the setting had been different, would the story have been different?
- Would you like to visit the setting of the book? If familiar with the setting, did it ring true?

Genre-Specific Book Club Questions

Nonfiction: Was the author able to convey things in an enjoyable way for a non-expert reader? Do you feel the author justified their conclusions? Do you feel the author provided an appropriate amount of information for the text?

Memoir: Were there gaps in the story you wish had been filled, or parts where you wished for less information? (If the book is fiction with biographical elements, why do you think the author chose to write the story in this way rather than as a memoir?)

Short Stories: Which story did you like best/least, and why? How are the stories connected? For example, what settings, themes, or characters do they share? Would you have liked to see any of these stories extended?

Historical Fiction: Do you feel the book was well-researched? Did you spot any anachronisms, or any period-specific aspect that wasn't mentioned but that you feel should have been?

Mysteries: When did you figure out "whodunnit"? What did you think of the red herrings the author inserted? Did you find them appropriate or forced? Was the ending satisfying?

General Book Club Topics Relating to the Book

- If you could start a movement in your community, what would it be? And why?
- Do you think it's true that we care less about others' opinions as we age?
- What are popular and favorite recipes of your family and region?
- Do you agree that "marriage is such a dreadful gamble"?
- Do you see the appeal of the [insert detail relevant to the book] lifestyle/career choice?

Example Exit Survey Email

Hi [First name],

I'm sorry to hear that you'll no longer be participating in the book club, we really enjoyed having you as part of the group. [Consider sharing a good memory].

I was wondering if you'd be willing to answer a few questions to help [us / me] improve the book club for members going forward? Please see the questions below, and no worries if there are any questions you'd like to skip.

1. Why are you leaving the book club?
2. How likely are you to recommend the book club to a friend, on a scale from 1-10?
3. What did you enjoy about the book club?
4. Is there anything you would change to make the club better?

Thanks again for being a member!

Acknowledgements

Thank you to all who've supported BookBrowse over the decades: first and foremost our members and member libraries who've funded us all these years; the survey participants who've provided us with their helpful insights; our editors and reviewers; and our founder, Davina Morgan-Witts.

Our Lead Editor Elisabeth Cook was instrumental in assembling the resources and adding supplemental sections for *A Club of One's One*, and our early readers Lisa Butts, Laurie McKenzie, Lana Maskus, Elizabeth of Silver's Reviews, Bridget Petrites, and Ashley Conte.

And of course, thank you to all who spend their time starting, planning, coordinating, facilitating, leading, and participating in book clubs—you make the world a better place.

Notes

[1] ESL Book Club – https://www.bookbrowse.com/featured-bookclubs/archives/index.cfm/bookclub_number/84

[2] C Facility Book Club – https://www.bookbrowse.com/featured-bookclubs/archives/index.cfm/bookclub_number/77

[3] Writers As Readers – https://www.bookbrowse.com/featured-bookclubs/archives/index.cfm/bookclub_number/59

[4] Zoom Black Girls' Book Club – https://www.bookbrowse.com/featured-bookclubs/archives/index.cfm/bookclub_number/79

[5] Books for Cooks – https://www.bookbrowse.com/featured-bookclubs/archives/index.cfm/bookclub_number/82

[6] Cross/Over Book Club – https://www.bookbrowse.com/featured-bookclubs/archives/index.cfm/bookclub_number/68

[7] Sistas Are Reading – https://www.bookbrowse.com/featured-bookclubs/archives/index.cfm/bookclub_number/86

[8] The Bibliophiles – https://www.bookbrowse.com/featured-bookclubs/archives/index.cfm/bookclub_number/72

[9] Girls' Night In Book Club – https://www.bookbrowse.com/featured-bookclubs/archives/index.cfm/bookclub_number/64

[10] 13 million adults – https://www.bookbrowse.com/blogs/editor/index.cfm/2025/5/16/How-many-people-are-in-a-book-club

[11] most popular books discussed that year – https://www.bookbrowse.com/blogs/editor/index.cfm/2025/4/3/The-Most-Popular-Book-Club-Books-of-2024

[12] Bookmovement.com – http://Bookmovement.com

[13] Bookclubs.com – http://Bookclubs.com

[14] its own platform – https://www.goodreads.com/group

[15] Bookclubs.com – http://Bookclubs.com

[16] Meetup – https://www.meetup.com/

[17] bookbrowse.com/onlinebookclub – http://bookbrowse.com/onlinebookclub

[18] bookbrowse.com/bchc – http://bookbrowse.com/bchc
[19] Top 10 Book Club Recommendations – https://www.bookbrowse.com/bookclubs/
[20] Award Winners – https://www.bookbrowse.com/awards/
[21] Libby – https://libbyapp.com/
[22] Bookshop.org – http://Bookshop.org
[23] Project Gutenberg – https://gutenberg.org/
[24] BookBub – https://www.bookbub.com/
[25] a search tool for finding lit mags – https://www.pw.org/literary_magazines
[26] LibriVox – https://librivox.org/
[27] reading guides – http://bookbrowse.com/reading_guides
[28] ChatGPT – https://chatgpt.com/
[29] So You Want to Talk About Race – https://www.bookbrowse.com/reviews/index.cfm/book_number/4119/so-you-want-to-talk-about-race
[30] on the BookBrowse website – https://www.bookbrowse.com/reading_guides/detail/index.cfm/book_number/4119/so-you-want-to-talk-about-race#reading_guide
[31] How to Read Now – https://www.bookbrowse.com/reviews/index.cfm/book_number/4483/how-to-read-now
[32] Facebook – https://www.facebook.com/
[33] Goodreads – https://www.goodreads.com/
[34] Facebook Messenger – https://www.messenger.com/
[35] WhatsApp – https://www.whatsapp.com/
[36] Facebook Messenger – https://www.messenger.com/
[37] Facebook Messenger – https://www.messenger.com/
[38] Zoom – https://www.zoom.com/
[39] Microsoft Teams – https://www.microsoft.com/en-us/microsoft-teams/group-chat-software
[40] Google Meet – https://meet.google.com/landing
[41] FaceTime – https://support.apple.com/en-us/105088
[42] Bel Canto Books – https://belcantobooks.net/about-us
[43] Goodreads maintains a database of virtual book groups – https://www.goodreads.com/group/show_tag/virtual-book-club
[44] BookClubs.com – https://bookclubs.com/join-a-book-club
[45] our current and past online discussions – https://www.bookbrowse.com/onlinebookclub/
[46] In an interview with BookBrowse – https://www.bookbrowse.com/featured-bookclubs/archives/index.cfm/bookclub_number/78
[47] Tasty One-Bite Appetizer Recipes –

https://www.tasteofhome.com/collection/one-bite-appetizer-recipes/

[48] Dishes to Wow Your Book Club – https://www.oprah.com/food/book-club-recipe-ideas/all

[49] Easy desserts for effortless entertaining – https://www.delicious.com.au/recipes/collections/gallery/60-easy-desserts-for-effortless-entertaining/77cijfrr

[50] list of recipes – https://www.tasteofhome.com/collection/recipes-for-book-club/

[51] Crying in H Mart – https://www.bookbrowse.com/bb_briefs/detail/index.cfm/ezine_preview_number/15676/crying-in-h-mart

[52] The Lost Apothecary – https://www.bookbrowse.com/reviews/index.cfm/book_number/4220/the-lost-apothecary

[53] Wild – https://www.bookbrowse.com/bb_briefs/detail/index.cfm/ezine_preview_number/7146/wild

[54] The Book Club CookBook – https://www.bookclubcookbook.com/

[55] Olive Kitteridge – https://www.bookbrowse.com/reviews/index.cfm/book_number/2257/olive-kitteridge

[56] So You Want to Talk About Race – https://www.bookbrowse.com/reviews/index.cfm/book_number/4119/so-you-want-to-talk-about-race

[57] The Henna Artist – https://www.bookbrowse.com/bb_briefs/detail/index.cfm/ezine_preview_number/14827/the-henna-artist

[58] A Gentleman in Moscow – https://www.bookbrowse.com/reviews/index.cfm/book_number/3454/a-gentleman-in-moscow

[59] The official website of historical fiction author Marie Benedict – https://www.authormariebenedict.com/book-clubs.html

[60] in an interview with BookBrowse – https://www.bookbrowse.com/featured-bookclubs/archives/index.cfm/bookclub_number/29

[61] YouTube – https://www.youtube.com/

[62] Playbill – https://playbill.com/

[63] The Personal Librarian – https://www.bookbrowse.com/reviews/index.cfm/book_number/4276

[64] Loving Frank – https://www.bookbrowse.com/reviews/index.cfm/book_number/2023

[65] Survey of Public Participation in the Arts – https://www.arts.gov/impact/research/publications/arts-participation-patterns-2022-

highlights-survey-public-participation-arts

[66] 2020 Census – https://www.census.gov/library/stories/2021/08/united-states-adult-population-grew-faster-than-nations-total-population-from-2010-to-2020.html

[67] bookbrowse.com/join – http://bookbrowse.com/join

[68] bookbrowse.com/join/free_signup.cfm – https://www.bookbrowse.com/join/free_signup.cfm

[69] cs@bookbrowse.com – mailto:cs@bookbrowse.com

[70] bookbrowse.com/bcref – http://bookbrowse.com/bcref

www.ingramcontent.com/pod-product-compliance
Lightning Source LLC
Chambersburg PA
CBHW060420300426
44111CB00018B/2921